Discovering the Michael Chekhov Technique

Discovering the Michael Chekhov Technique

In the Studio with Ted Pugh and Fern Sloan

Danielle Carter

methuen | drama
LONDON • NEW YORK • OXFORD • NEW DELHI • SYDNEY

METHUEN DRAMA
Bloomsbury Publishing Plc, 50 Bedford Square, London, WC1B 3DP, UK
Bloomsbury Publishing Inc, 1385 Broadway, New York, NY 10018, USA
Bloomsbury Publishing Ireland, 29 Earlsfort Terrace, Dublin 2, D02 AY28, Ireland

BLOOMSBURY, METHUEN DRAMA and the Methuen Drama logo are
trademarks of Bloomsbury Publishing Plc

First published in Great Britain 2026

Copyright © Danielle Carter, 2026

Danielle Carter has asserted her right under the Copyright, Designs and Patents
Act, 1988, to be identified as Author of this work.

For legal purposes the Acknowledgements on pp. 183–4 constitute an extension
of this copyright page.

Cover design: Ben Anslow
Cover image: Creamsicle Dreams © Aaron Reed

All rights reserved. No part of this publication may be: i) reproduced or
transmitted in any form, electronic or mechanical, including photocopying,
recording or by means of any information storage or retrieval system without
prior permission in writing from the publishers; or ii) used or reproduced in
any way for the training, development or operation of artificial intelligence (AI)
technologies, including generative AI technologies. The rights holders expressly
reserve this publication from the text and data mining exception as per Article
4(3) of the Digital Single Market Directive (EU) 2019/790.

Bloomsbury Publishing Plc does not have any control over, or responsibility for,
any third-party websites referred to or in this book. All internet addresses given
in this book were correct at the time of going to press. The author and publisher
regret any inconvenience caused if addresses have changed or sites have ceased
to exist, but can accept no responsibility for any such changes.

A catalogue record for this book is available from the British Library.

A catalog record for this book is available from the Library of Congress.

ISBN: HB: 978-1-3503-2060-4
PB: 978-1-3503-2059-8
ePDF: 978-1-3503-2062-8
eBook: 978-1-3503-2061-1

Typeset by Deanta Global Publishing Services, Chennai, India
Printed and bound in Great Britain

For product safety related questions contact productsafety@bloomsbury.com.

To find out more about our authors and books visit www.bloomsbury.com
and sign up for our newsletters.

To Michael Chekhov, Ted Pugh, Fern Sloan and Ragnar Freidank for giving me new ground on which to stand

As actors and actresses, we must rejoice in the possession of our physical faculties. We must experience joy in the use of our hands, arms, body, etc. Without this appreciation and realization of the body and its many possibilities, we cannot perform as artists. You should feel a flow of joy because you are alive. Your body will feel full of life. That is what you must give from the stage. Your life. No less. That is art: to give all you have. And what have you? Your life – nothing more. And to give life means to feel life throughout your whole being.

Michael Chekhov
13 April 1936
Lessons for Teachers, Lesson III

CONTENTS

List of figures xii
Biographies xiii
Foreword xv
A note from Ted Pugh and Fern Sloan xvii
Preface xix

Part 1: Introduction: Origins of the Chekhov work 1
    The Dartington ladies 1
    Ted Pugh 3
    Fern Sloan 5
    The collaboration begins 5
    From students to teachers 6
    The Actors' Ensemble 7
    The Chekhov work today 8
    Why pursue a technique at all? The Chekhov
       perspective 8

Part 2: The essentials 11
    Laying the foundation: key terms and concepts 11
        Listening to the body 12
        The psycho-physical 13
        Images 15
        Tangible and intangible 16
        Sensing and thinking 17
        The inspired state 17
    Crossing the threshold 18
    Expanding and contracting 19
    The actor's ideal centre 22

The qualities of movement 23
    A note on terminology: 'radiating' 24
    Transitions between the qualities of movement
        and moments of change 24
    Qualities of movement and parts of the body 25
The four brothers 26
    Ease 26
    Form 27
    Beauty 27
    A feeling of the whole 28
    The four brothers together: bring your unknowing into
        being 28
Radiating and receiving 29
    Radiating 29
    Receiving 30
    Radiating and receiving together 31
    Throwing a ball to understand radiating
        and receiving 32
    The technique of radiating and receiving 33
The three physical centres – thinking, feeling and will 34
Directions 36
    Front-space and back-space 37
    In and out 38
    Directions and gesture 40
    How to use direction in developing a character 40
    A Practical Application for Directions: The First Pass
        at a Script 41
    Trajectories 41
    Final points on directions 42

Part 3: Transformative tools 45

    Imaginary centres 46
        Choosing your imaginary centre 47
        Working with imaginary centres 47
        Moving and changing centres 48
    Staccato and legato 50
        The polarity of staccato and legato 51
        Using staccato and legato to fill out a character 51

Inner and outer tempo 53
Quality and sensation 54
    Large packages of feelings/sensations and our personal feelings 55
    Through the will 56
Atmosphere 57
    Objective atmospheres 58
    Personal atmosphere 59
    Personal atmosphere and objective atmosphere 59
    How to create an atmosphere 60
Imaginary body 61
    Playing with imaginary bodies 62
    Moments of change with imaginary body 63
Archetype 64
    Listening in to the archetype 65
    Deciding on an archetype 65
Psychological gesture 69
    The difference between movement and gesture 69
    How to develop a psychological gesture 69
    How to use psychological gesture 72

Part 4: Putting the tools to use 75

The first read of a play 78
Working with images 79
Layering the tools 80
Working with limited time 84
Camera work 85
Moments of change 86
Bringing the technique onto the stage 86

Part 5: Class exercises 89

The essentials 90
    Expanding and contracting – a beginner's class 90
Expanding and contracting – advanced 93
Opening and closing gestures, or expanding and contracting? 94
Qualities of movement – a beginner's class 96

Moulding (earth) 96
Floating (water) 98
Flying (air) 99
Radiating (fire) 100
Qualities of movement – advanced 102
    Exercise 1 102
    Exercise 2 102
    Exercise 3 103
Four brothers – a beginner's class 103
Four brothers – advanced 106
Radiating and receiving 107
    Exercise 1 107
    Exercise 2 109
    Exercise 3 110
    Exercise 4 111
Touch and contact 112
The three centres 114
Directions 117
    Front 117
    Back 119
    In and out 121
    Down 123
    Up 124
    Trajectories 125
Transformative tools 126
    Imaginary centres 126
Straight lines and curves with imaginary centres 128
Staccato and legato 132
Qualities of movement with tempo 135
Sensation with tempo 137
Quality and sensation 139
    Quality and sensation through straight line and curved line 143
Personal atmosphere 145
Ensemble and objective atmosphere 149
Imaginary body 151
Stick, ball, veil 155

Archetypes 158
Awakening to gesture 160
    Exercise 1 161
    Exercise 2 162
    Exercise 3 162
    Exercise 4 165
Psychological gesture – adding quality and objective 165
Using a mask to explore archetypal gestures 167
Choices, contact and point of focus 168
An exercise for the last week of class: an invitation 170

Part 6: Some guidance for teaching the Chekhov work 173

Misconceptions about the Chekhov technique 174
Beginning a class: training actors to become
    receptive 174
Teaching focus and concentration 175
Working with young actors 176
Teaching non-actors 177
Teaching images 177
Teaching imaginary body, imaginary centre
    and gesture 178
On using balls as a teaching aid 179
Wrapping up 180
In conclusion 182

Acknowledgements 183
References 187
Web addresses 189
Index 190

LIST OF FIGURES

1	Contraction, 2016. By Val Kissel	20
2	Expanding, 2016. By Val Kissel	21
3	The Actor's Ideal Centre, 2016. By Val Kissel	23
4	Ted Pugh, 2018. Photography by Jessica Maynard	33
5	Staccato and Legato, 2016. By Val Kissel	51
6	Staccato and Legato II, 2016. By Val Kissel	52
7	The Distance Travelled, 2015. Photography by Danielle Carter	172
8	Fern Sloan, 2015. Photography by Peggy Coffey	172
9	Fern Sloan, 2015. Photography by Edward Marritz	184
10	Fern Sloan, 2021. Photography by Ragnar Freidank	185
11	Ragnar Freidank, 2015. Photography by Eddie Marritz	185
12	Ted Pugh, 2018. Photography Jessica Maynard	186
13	Ted Pugh, 2018. Photography Jessica Maynard	186
14	Danielle Carter, 2015. Photography by Edward Marritz	189

BIOGRAPHIES

Fern Sloan discovered she was an actress in 1960 and has been pursuing the art ever since. After performing as a leading lady in regional theatres and off-Broadway, she was introduced to the work of Michael Chekhov. She was certified by Beatrice Straight and taught at the Michael Chekhov Studio in New York City. She is co-founder and co-director of the Actors' Ensemble and the Michael Chekhov School in Hudson, New York, from which she has travelled and taught actors around the world. Her primary interest has been to develop the actors' performance skills and abilities and get this work on to the stage.

Ted Pugh began his professional career at Washington DC's Arena Stage. As an actor, he has appeared on Broadway, off-Broadway and at regional theatres across the country. He is co-founder and co-director of the Actors' Ensemble and was a student and teacher at the Michael Chekhov Studio in New York City for seven years, certified as a teacher by Beatrice Straight and Deirdre Hurst du Prey in 1983. He has taught workshops throughout the US, Europe, Croatia and the former Soviet Union. He is co-director of the Michael Chekhov School in Hudson, New York.

Joanna Merlin was the last surviving student of Michael Chekhov and the founder and president of MICHA. She was a faculty member at New York University's Graduate Acting programme. She played opposite Laurence Olivier in *Becket* and originated the role of Tzeitel in *Fiddler on the Roof*. Her films include *Class Action*, *Mystic Pizza*, *Fame* and *The Ten Commandments*. On TV, she played Judge Petrovsky on *Law and Order SVU* for 11 seasons. She was the casting director for Harold Prince, Stephen Sondheim, Bernardo Bertolucci, Michael Cimino and James Ivory. She is a co-founder of the Alliance for Inclusion in the Arts and was a member of the Tony Awards Nominating Committee. Her book *Auditioning: An Actor-Friendly Guide*, published in 2001, is still in print. Joanna passed away in October 2023 at the age of 92.

Bethany Caputo is an actor, acting coach and Chekhov teacher in NYC. She has performed at regional theatres across the country, such as the Goodman and Arena Stage, and on television. Ms Caputo studied at the Moscow Art Theatre and is on faculty with the Michael Chekhov Association, where she was an actor for *Master Classes in the Michael Chekhov Technique* and is now director of the Michael Chekhov Studio in NYC and co-artistic director, with Ted and Fern, of the Actors' Ensemble. She has taught at universities in the US, such as NYU: TISCH School of Arts, and abroad in Zurich, Shanghai, Melbourne and Sydney. She can be found at bethanycaputo.com.

Ragnar Freidank trained as an actor in his native Germany and since 2004 has been teaching acting in New York. He has been on the faculty of Columbia University, Sarah Lawrence College, Brooklyn College, Marymount Manhattan College, Michael Howard Studios and The New School, and teaches his own Scene-Class. In 2015 he co-founded the Michael Chekhov School of Acting in Hudson, New York, with Fern Sloan and Ted Pugh. He works as a freelance theatre director, filmmaker, location sound-recordist, camera operator and editor. He directed the award-winning narrative film *Beautiful Hills of Brooklyn*, starring Joanna Merlin; the executive producer was Bob Balaban. He co-directed the acclaimed DVD series *Master Classes in the Michael Chekhov Technique*, produced by the Michael Chekhov Association (MICHA). He made the *D&D Roadshow Movie* for Improbable Theatre (UK) and most recently collaborated on *Tao of Glass*, with Phelim McDermott and composer Philip Glass.

FOREWORD

This book is a gift to all those interested in exploring the Michael Chekhov technique. It is filled with the advice, lessons and wisdom of Fern Sloan and Ted Pugh, two great teachers of the Michael Chekhov technique. Great teachers are rare. They love what they're teaching. They never stop learning, exploring and experimenting. They raise the bar. They inspire.

I first met Ted and Fern in the 1980s when I taught at the Michael Chekhov Studio in New York City. It is my good fortune to have been their close friend and colleague since that time. They were part of the founding faculty of the Michael Chekhov Association (MICHA). Their experiential teaching has enriched our work in immeasurable ways since MICHA's inception.

As the last surviving student of Michael Chekhov, I feel that Fern and Ted embody Chekhov's spirit and psycho-physical approach. In addition to being artists in the deepest sense, they are visionary, generous, open and exuberant. They are beloved by their students and all who know them. They have been working together as a team for so many years that they form their own ensemble, bonded yet separate in their embrace of the process.

The Chekhov work continues to excite them, which radiates to their students. Though they are in their eighties, their dedicated practice has allowed them to maintain their physical strength and abilities. They move as though they were still young, an amazing phenomenon to behold!

The Michael Chekhov School in Hudson, upstate New York, was the brilliant idea of Ted Pugh and Fern Sloan, together with Ragnar Freidank. The school has flourished since they opened the doors. Actors, teachers and students come from all over the world to study with these actors. Some participants have translated Michael Chekhov's books into their own language as a result of Ted, Fern and Ragnar's inspired teaching.

Danielle Carter met Fern and Ted at MICHA's annual workshop in Connecticut and subsequently travelled back several times from Australia to continue her studies with them at the Hudson School. In this book, she has made an enormous contribution to the understanding and practice of Michael Chekhov's work. As a result, their years of voracious curiosity and discovery will belong forever to the art of acting training.

Joanna Merlin (1931–2023)
2022

A NOTE FROM TED PUGH AND FERN SLOAN

We have been developing our approach to Michael Chekhov's work for over forty years. We consider ourselves still to be on a path of discovery. In *To the Actor*, Michael Chekhov himself told actors that he needed their help.[1] This is a generous invitation to develop our own individual approaches to his work.

How do you translate a living process of exploration and investigation, filled with inner and outer movement, into words on a page? In participating in Danielle Carter's response to that challenge, we have had to delve deeper into articulating what it is we do.

As theatre artists, we are engaged in seeking what lies behind the words: what brings life to the image, to the imagination. The work Chekhov has given us has endless possibilities. To learn how to use tools that seek to uncover, illuminate and reveal what lies hidden within each individual is the task of a lifetime. We are constantly questioning how best to bring these tools to life. It is a joyful task, as hidden secrets are revealed and deeper levels are made available to us.

In making available our years of investigating and practising this work, we hope that we might be of help to others: to clarify, encourage and perhaps even inspire those in pursuit of a better understanding of the legacy left to us by Michael Chekhov.

---

[1] Michael Chekhov, *To the Actor on the Technique of Acting* (London: Routledge, 2002), LIII.

The Chekhov method or technique has found its way through the world, in universities, colleges and private studios and among individuals seeking to free their creative imagination. Its appeal is to bring wholeness to the human being, free of the media.

A great variety of approaches to Chekhov's legacy have developed over the years. This is ours.

Danielle Carter has our heartfelt gratitude for initiating and carrying this book from beginning to end. Without her expertise and support, this would never have come about.

Ted Pugh and Fern Sloan 2022

PREFACE

In the year 2013, I was struggling. My professional life as an actor was characterized by the nagging feeling that something was missing. I felt like I was *seeking*: inspiration, transformation and a more dynamic way of working. The choices I was making felt narrow. The way I went about shaping a character and telling a story felt flat. Simply put, my toolbox felt limited.

That year, an opportunity came up: to study acting in the United States of America. It had been twenty years since I had studied intensively in an acting classroom. Would this training be the missing element I had been looking for? Unfortunately, it wasn't. It did, nevertheless, introduce me to the work of Michael Chekhov. For me, he became the bright, brilliant light on that voyage. I sensed I was on the precipice of something. I wasn't quite sure what, but I knew that I had been unmoored, bewitched and intrigued by Chekhov's work. I was curious. I vowed that my next study trip would be a deep dive into the Chekhov technique.

I waited two years for that odyssey to begin. In 2015, Ted Pugh, Fern Sloan and Ragnar Freidank entered my life, at the newly formed Michael Chekhov School in Hudson, New York. That summer changed my life as an actor – as did the summers that followed, as I continued to investigate and explore Chekhov's techniques with Ted, Fern and Ragnar. An experiential acting method was revealed to me: I discovered new tools to play with and a fresh, innovative way of seeing, creating and working in the world. Never had I entered a room that was so unequivocally gentle, experiential and creative – yet demanded such rigour. I noticed that, with each passing summer, my work became richer, deeper and freer.

Fern Sloan and Ted Pugh are extraordinary educators, and they are unique in their collaborative teaching approach. They hold the space for actors to work, listening to students, to the space and to each other while guiding or observing. They teach collaboratively, and their style is kind, rigorous and playful. They continue to peel back the layers of Chekhov's work, finding more and more the longer they explore it. Even now, in their eighties, they tell me, they still feel like children in this sense.

For Ted and Fern as actors and also as teachers, uncovering the inexhaustible levels of meaning revealed through Michael Chekhov's work is a constant source of new life. Seeking to penetrate the physical/tangible with non-tangible realities is indeed the work of a lifetime. That specific process of learning, seeking and uncovering, using the tools Chekhov gave us, is referred to throughout this book as 'the Chekhov work'. It's a term used by students and teachers of this technique worldwide.

On my part, Fern's and Ted's teaching gave rise to new opportunities to investigate, research and discover the limitless capacities within the human organism: the wonder of the physical form and the wisdom of the body. There is nothing about the Chekhov work that's not engaging. It offers the actor the possibility of being an artist. Every moment is an exploration, full with the riches of seeking and discovering.

In this book, I seek both to honour Ted and Fern and to share the gifts I have received from them – an invaluable legacy – with the world. If I have fulfilled my aim, this book will serve as a testament to what they have dedicated to this work, and to the many actors who now practise it.

This book is the result of many hours spent with Fern and Ted, on the floor, in discussion with them and recording and observing them at work. I hope that my own experience as an actor now trained in the Chekhov work has qualified me to translate my observations into the words that appear on these pages. The ideas, the experience, and the knowledge here are Fern's and Ted's; my part has been to crystallize that expertise into the sentences, paragraphs and chapters that make up this book. (It's a transformation that reflects and honours, perhaps, that transformation an actor is always seeking to achieve, in taking an aspect of shared human experience and presenting it in a new shape or form.)

I hope that this book allows you to hear the voices of these master teachers who have devoted their days to discovering and developing Chekhov's technique. I hope that, in this way, you will profit from what Ted and Fern have spent a lifetime unearthing.

I have chosen to focus primarily on Fern's and Ted's more traditional teachings of the Chekhov work for this book. Ragnar Freidank, who works with Fern and Ted, takes a unique approach to the work that is almost impossible to capture on the page.

The book is loosely divided into early parts covering theory and later parts covering practice.

- Part 1 gives a brief history of the Chekhov work in general and Ted's and Fern's work in particular.
- Part 2 covers key terms and concepts and then sets out the essential tools.
- Part 3 expands on these essentials, presenting a set of transformational tools.
- In Part 4, we move towards the practical; this part is informed by Ted and Fern's own experience in discussing how actors might begin to put these tools to use.
- Part 5 sets out transcripts of actual classes run by Ted and Fern. Bethany Caputo takes the class on directions. Student actors – and teachers of such groups – will find these directly useful in their own practice.
- Part 6 is specifically for teachers of the Chekhov work; it shares Ted's and Fern's insights on guiding others in this intuitive creative process.

This book is primarily for actors, not for scholars. It's about *doing* the work, not discussing the work. It's about applying a specific set of tools to unearth and create a character; it's about exploring the text and world of a play and digging deep into moments of change. It is a handbook for actors that serves as a complete introduction to the Chekhov technique. Ultimately, it's an invitation to engage with your own creative individuality.

This book is the Michael Chekhov technique seen through the lens of Fern Sloan and Ted Pugh, two master teachers who have followed their curiosity and spent over half their lives exploring, investigating and experimenting with this unique body of work.

Danielle Carter 2024

Part 1

Introduction

Origins of the Chekhov work

Actor, director and author Michael Chekhov was born in Russia in 1891, and died in California in 1955. He was considered by many to be one of the greatest actors of the twentieth century. A nephew of seminal playwright Anton Chekhov, he was also one of the most influential acting teachers in twentieth-century theatre practice. His impact on generations of actors (including Yul Brynner, Clint Eastwood, Anthony Hopkins, Jack Nicholson and Marilyn Monroe, among many others) was profound.

Astonishingly, Chekhov's ground-breaking method came perilously close to disappearing into obscurity in his lifetime. The 'psycho-physical' approach that he developed – coming to your feelings through movement, through the will, through image – was rejected in his home country of Russia during his lifetime. If it hadn't been for the 'Dartington ladies' – in particular, Deirdre Hurst du Prey and Beatrice Straight – his ideas might not have come to light at all.

The Dartington ladies

Beatrice Straight, born in 1914, was the daughter of Willard Straight and Dorothy Payne Whitney, then one of the richest women in the world. After Willard Straight died, Dorothy married philanthropist Leonard Elmhirst, and together they bought Dartington Hall, a fourteenth-century estate on the River Dart in Devon, England.

There they established a progressive school and aimed to develop a refuge for the world's best artists, including dancers, sculptors, painters, actors and playwrights.

In *Dartington Hall: The formative years*,[1] Victor Bonham-Carter writes that the school's 'distinctiveness lay in the emphasis placed upon the arts and crafts, upon projects, and non-academic subjects, upon ideas about self-expression and self-government'.

Beatrice herself was a student at the school when she first met Deirdre Hurst du Prey. Deirdre and Beatrice took classes together in music, art, puppetry and dance. In 1935, they travelled to America, at the Elmhirsts' request, to find an acting teacher and director for Dartington Hall School.

In New York, Deirdre and Beatrice saw Michael Chekhov performing at the Majestic Theatre. 'We were absolutely thunderstruck', Deirdre later recalled of the experience. 'We could never have imagined seeing acting of the kind that evening.'[2]

Michael Chekhov first studied acting under Konstantin Stanislavski at the First Studio at the Moscow Arts Theatre, where he had become a favoured student, acting, directing and studying Stanislavski's 'system'. In 1922, he became director of the First Studio. After the October Revolution in 1917, Chekhov began touring with his own company, developing his own theories.

In the 1920s, Chekhov had come into conflict with the Communist regime. In 1928, he fled Russia and emigrated to Germany. Between 1928 and 1935 he worked in Vienna, Berlin, Paris and Lithuania, studying, performing, directing and teaching.

Chekhov accepted the Elmhirsts' invitation to establish the Chekhov Theatre School in Dartington in 1936. At Dartington Hall, he began to put on paper his ideas about what theatre and acting could be.

The prospect of war in 1938 made it impossible for Chekhov's school to continue in Dartington. By December that year, the school had effectively moved to Ridgefield, Connecticut in the United

---

[1]Victor Bonham-Carter, *Dartington Hall: The Formative Years: 1925–1957* (Dulverton, Somerset: The Exmoor Press, 1970), 46.
[2]Diane Caracciolo, 'Deirdre Hurst Du Prey: A Life Devoted to the Creative Imagination', in *The Swing of the Pendulum: The Urgency of Arts Education for Healing, Learning and Wholeness*, ed. Diane Caracciolo and Courtney Lee Weider (Rotterdam: SensePublishers, 1999).

States, where it became the Chekhov Studio. The first six graduates received diplomas in October 1939. That month, the Chekhov Studio players presented *The Possessed* (by George Shdanoff, based on Dostoyevsky's novel) on Broadway.

The Chekhov Studio players had successful American repertory tours in 1940–1941 but the Second World War greatly reduced the number of available male actors. The original Chekhov Studio in the United States was formally closed in 1942. At that point, Michael Chekhov moved to Los Angeles, where he was offered various film roles. Most memorably, he appeared as the Freudian analyst in Alfred Hitchcock's *Spellbound* in 1945 (for which he received an Oscar nomination).

Chekhov had published his own description of his acting technique, *On the Technique of Acting*, in 1942. An abridged version appeared as *To the Actor* in 1953, two years before his death. The book sat on shelves in university libraries for years, gathering dust. But in 1977, interest in Chekhov was sparked when Beatrice Straight won an Oscar for Best Supporting Actress in the film *Network* and thanked Chekhov as her teacher and mentor in her acceptance speech.

Thereafter, Beatrice was inundated with requests to open a studio where actors could learn the Chekhov technique. In 1980, she established the Michael Chekhov Studio in New York, along with Deirdre Hurst du Prey and two other 'Dartington ladies', Eleanor Faison and Felicity Mason. All had studied with Chekhov at Dartington Hall between 1936 and 1938.

In the 1980s, this second Chekhov Studio was the only place one could study the Chekhov technique with teachers who had learnt from Chekhov himself. One of the studio's early students was Ted Pugh.

Ted Pugh

Ted Pugh was introduced to the work of Michael Chekhov in 1957 when he was a theatre student at the University of Oklahoma. His best friend at the time, Ron Thompson, had gifted him Chekhov's *To the Actor*. Ted took the book with him to the Cape Playhouse in Dennis, Massachusetts, where he had been cast in summer stock. At that time, he told me, he wasn't sure he really understood the book; the one thing he does remember is its focus on imagination.

Ted got his theatre degree, was drafted into the army for two years and then spent six months at the Arena Stage theatre in Washington, DC. From there he made his way to New York City, where, in 1962, he auditioned for the renowned acting teacher Uta Hagen and was accepted into her class. He remembers looking at *To the Actor* often during this time. He talked to actor friends about his wish to find someone who could teach them the technique, but somehow it never worked out.

When Uta Hagen went to London with *Who's Afraid of Virginia Woolf?* Ted found a new teacher, Michael Howard, who had himself been taught by Sanford Meisner of the Neighbourhood Playhouse and Lee Strasberg of the Actors Studio. Ted's training at the University of Oklahoma had been primarily classical; now he was immersed in the Method technique. There was a lot of the Method that Ted wasn't comfortable with. He didn't want to get up in front of a class and portray private moments; he found that embarrassing. Michael advised him to 'Use what works for you, and if it doesn't, don't do it'.

Ted established a career in theatre and television, appearing on and off Broadway and at regional theatres across the country. However, he began to feel uninspired. He took a year off to study at the Christian Community Seminary in Stuttgart, Germany. When he came back, he says, it was with the sole purpose of finding out how to continue.

In 1981, he found the answer he had been seeking when a friend told him about the newly formed Michael Chekhov Studio. Ted, then forty-two, successfully auditioned as a student. His Chekhov journey had begun in earnest.

As Ted tells it, at that point he went right to the centre of the Chekhov work. He doesn't claim that his work at the beginning of this journey was advanced, but he does feel that this was the point at which the door flung open for him. He had longed for an availability to his emotional life that wasn't invasive and emotionally disturbing. Through the medium of the psychophysical, this suddenly felt closer at hand.

Ted now believes that an actor is never finished with the Chekhov work. One is always learning he says; always in the process of becoming. The more we take that in and see that as the goal itself, the happier and healthier we will be as actors and as human beings.

Fern Sloan

Fern's story is a little different. In 1960, aged twenty-five, she arrived in New York City from Kansas, hoping to carve out a career as a singer. Her singing teacher told her that to be a professional singer, she would need to know something about acting, so she sought out training, taking night classes at the American Academy of Dramatic Arts while working full time as a typist. Having embarked on these classes, Fern soon realized that she was an actor, not a singer.

Fern was given leading roles at the Academy and was awarded a full-time scholarship for the second year. However, when she graduated, she didn't feel she had a strong technique. She told me that at that point she knew she was operating solely on intuition. To this end, she went in search of further study: first with Walt Witcover at the HB Studio and then, for several years, with Uta Hagen.

At that time in her life, *Fern says*, she would spend hours analysing a text and filling books with notes. She related personally to the characters, the situations, the relationships. It was a lot of 'headwork' she says; although the headwork, as she put it, 'went right into my emotional life'.

Although she managed to find regular work in the theatre, performing as a leading lady in regional theatres and off-Broadway, Fern felt limited by this way of working – drawing on personal experience only – that she had arrived at. As a consequence, she left the theatre.

The collaboration begins

Fern Sloan met Ted Pugh through the work of Rudolf Steiner, the early twentieth-century philosopher, spiritual scientist, and founder of Anthroposophy – which had grown out of theosophy, and centred on human development. The two already knew each other the day that Ted invited Fern to have a cup of tea with him to discuss the work of Michael Chekhov – who had also been an Anthroposophist. At that point, Fern didn't know who Michael Chekhov was. As she describes the meeting, 'it was a nice invitation to have tea with a nice man'.

Soon after this meeting, Ted helped organize a public acting workshop in New York City led by another Anthroposophist, the English actor and teacher Peter Bridgmont. Fern took the workshop. In participating, she says, she recognized that much of her being had been laid to rest during her hiatus from acting. It was the first time in several years that she had dared venture back into theatre. It was a major turning point in her creative life.

After this workshop, Ted suggested that Fern drop in on a Chekhov class he was teaching. Fern went, and that was it: the penny dropped. She couldn't believe such a technique existed. As Fern puts it, 'I fell in love with the Chekhov work one Friday afternoon at the Rudolf Steiner School in New York City in a class taught by Ted Pugh'. She had an immediate response to the work. It was as if she already knew what it was, she says; her body and being were available to it, and it was available to her. The consciousness that was required in the attempt to fulfil and to embody various parts of the work was deeply satisfying to her; she felt that new worlds had been made available. Through this work, Fern was brought more in tune with the essence of her own being.

From students to teachers

One of Ted's teachers at the Chekhov Studio was Eddie Grove, who had studied with Chekhov during his last few years in California. Ted told me that it was Eddie who put Chekhov's *To the Actor* 'in my bones'.

Eddie Grove clashed with Blair Cutting, the first director of the Michael Chekhov Studio, and eventually left the studio, taking his students with him. They rented a space two doors down and started the Michael Chekhov Study Centre. However, the new class itself soon clashed with Eddie too. Class members asked Ted – who was older than the other students and had a twenty-year career in theatre and television under his belt – to take over. He agreed.

Beatrice Straight, Deidre Hurst du Prey, Eleanor Faison and Felicity Mason – the Dartington ladies – asked Ted and his students to return to the original Chekhov Studio after watching the students perform *Spoon River Anthology* in the basement of the Fifth Avenue Presbyterian Church in New York City. They all agreed. Ted was certified as a teacher by Beatrice Straight and Deirdre Hurst du Prey in 1983. He taught at the Chekhov Studio for the last several years of its existence.

Fern, too, was certified by Beatrice Straight and served on the faculty for three years. The studio closed in 1990; Beatrice Straight was at that point suffering from Alzheimer's disease. Its legacy, however, lives on.

The Actors' Ensemble

In 1984, Ted and Fern, along with Charles Harper, formed the pioneering theatre company The Actors' Ensemble, inspired by their love for the Chekhov technique. The Ensemble's vision was, and still is, to investigate and research the Michael Chekhov work and to put that work on the stage. In particular, the Ensemble aimed to develop the art of the actor, independent of sets, costumes, lighting designers and anything else other than the acting process. Process, for Ted and Fern, has been everything.

The Ensemble has never been afraid to experiment. The three original actors – who became four with the addition of Glen Williamson – were happy just to be in a room together, trying things out.

Since its formation, the Ensemble has had many permutations, but the underlying principles have remained the same: practising, exploring and investigating what it means to put a story on the stage; allowing choices to reveal themselves rather than being imposed. 'Choice should liberate you', *Fern says*. 'Curiosity is insatiable.'

Ted, too, embraces the freedom of trusting the work. 'There is something basic about the work itself that always challenges, nourishes and surprises', he says.

All the actors who have worked with Fern and Ted over the years in the Ensemble have been guided by their interest in the Chekhov work. It sounds like a narrow focus, but it isn't. The Chekhov technique provides an actor with the tools to work with themselves as a human being – with their humanity. That, Ted and Fern believe, can be researched forever.

The Chekhov work today

Fern and Ted continued to teach the Chekhov work in various contexts, including New York University and the Sunbridge College (which provides courses inspired by Anthroposophy), throughout the 1990s. In 1999, the Michael Chekhov Association (MICHA) opened, and the pair began to teach there. In 2015, alongside Ragnar Freidank, they opened the Michael Chekhov School in Hudson, New York. Fern and Ted had been pioneers of what gradually became a Chekhov movement. For this, their particular expertise has always been in demand.

Through MICHA, Chekhov is studied in many universities in the United States, and there are Michael Chekhov Studios throughout the world.

As of 2024, Chekhov's work is being taught, researched and practised in Canada, England, Turkey, Egypt, Israel, Brazil, Thailand, Taiwan, Croatia, Serbia, China, Japan, Australia, many European countries and, prominently, in the United States.

So, what is the potential of this work that Michael Chekhov has left us? And how can we bring it to life on the stage?

Why pursue a technique at all? The Chekhov perspective

Ted and Fern believe that technique frees our creative potential: the chambers within us that are waiting to be accessed. Through technique, we seek to expand our capacity and to go beyond our familiar feelings. A solid technique enables an actor to be free, to transform and to inspire. Gifted actors, Chekhov himself said, need a technique.[3]

---

[3] *To the Actor*, 154–61.

As actors, we need to learn a technique and then forget it. We tend to forget it too soon. You have to permeate your whole being with technique, Fern and Ted believe, so that the technique can play you, rather than the other way round. Some actors have an impressive technique, but the result doesn't move you; the actor hasn't got to that place where they can loosen their grip and allow things to happen. When you craft something, there is a difference between letting it have life and holding on tightly to the craft. You can't freely do this work until it is a part of your body's language; until it's truly available to you.

Fern and Ted understand that technique will release you. It's there to free you, not to control you. An actor needs an instrument – the body – that is open and available. The joy of being an actor is the joy of going into the unknown: opening, releasing, uncovering, revealing humanity's depth and scope.

As an actor, you can travel on God-given talent for a time, but that talent will ultimately diminish without technique.

When technique has become a part of your body's language, you will find that in a performance, you can trust your instrument. You know what it is, what it needs to do, and you let it be and trust it, every night. Even so, there will be other times at which you may have to back up a little bit and reconnect with technique.

A combination of technique, ability and spontaneity is what an artist relies on to create a piece of art: 'art must be based on technique'.[4]

---

[4] Michael Chekhov, 'Lesson Given After Performance at Dartington of Uday Shankar and His Company of Dancers and Musicians', 6 October 1936, https://collections.uwindsor.ca/chekhov/item/595.

Part 2

The essentials

This part will introduce you to the potential of the Chekhov technique.

We begin with the essentials as they appear in the exercises Chekhov describes in the first chapter of his book *To the Actor*:

- expanding and contracting
- the ideal centre
- the qualities of movement: moulding, floating, flying, radiating
- the four brothers: ease, form, beauty and a sense of the whole
- radiating and receiving

Fern and Ted add to this list two further essentials:

- directions
- the three physical centres: the will, the head and the chest (known as the ideal centre)

Laying the foundation: key terms and concepts

Before we take a deep dive into these essentials, let's discuss some key terms and concepts that Ted and Fern often talk about:

- listening to the body
- the psycho-physical

- sensations
- images
- tangible and intangible
- sensing and thinking
- the inspired state

Like many aspects of the Chekhov work, coming to grips with these concepts will take time and practice. Allow yourself this time.

Listening to the body

Through the Chekhov technique, we relearn our relationship to our body. This approach to acting is experiential. If you don't experience it with your whole self – heart, body and soul – you will not understand the language or the technique. The Chekhov technique is grounded in the relationship of body and movement to the soul life. In this way, it offers untold inspiration.

When we talk about listening to the body, we are talking about awareness through movement. The way to start is by simply being aware of what is happening with your physical body. We are aiming to become very conscious that there is an echo, a reverberation, something moving within us. Listen to the form that the body has taken; listen after you've made a gesture. When you engage in an activity, consciously ask yourself what it is that you have awakened from that activity. What plays back upon you? Did something happen in you that you haven't experienced before? Is your perception of the space different? Is your perception of another different? Are you tense? Are you at ease? Are you tired? Don't resist those feelings; just be aware of what is going on for you. Give yourself time to begin to become aware.

Listening can be obvious or subtle. It's not just about listening to your individual body and process. We can listen in to the space, to our acting partners or to the space between. We can listen in to the ensemble.

If you find this hard, begin by ringing a bell. See how long you can keep listening, even after the sound seems to diminish. How long can you continue to listen, even though the bell sound is not there anymore? Can you extend your capacity for listening to other things in the same way? Give yourself over to listening.

You will find the exercises in this book easier if you are always moving towards a place of greater openness and ease. In this way, you will receive the exercises in a much more unconscious and thorough way. The key to this is to train yourself to listen with ease.

An actor should approach the Chekhov work, always, with ease as a foundation.

The psycho-physical

In *To the Actor*, Chekhov says the actor must strive for 'complete balance or harmony between the body and psychology'.[1] We must think of our bodies as our instruments for expressing creative ideas; we will return to this idea throughout this book. The term 'psycho-physical', which you will also continually encounter throughout this book and books about Michael Chekhov and his methodology, refers to the connection between the inner and outer, the physical self and the inner self, the body and the feeling/emotional life.

In practising the Chekhov technique, when you do something physically, you then observe what is happening inwardly. You are always seeking how the exercises relate to your inner life.

Through movement, you can awaken something in the inner life that plays with the outer life, so that there is no separation between the two. The inner life and the outer life play: they are constantly in dialogue. The body speaks; that which lives inside you is allowed to express itself through the physical body.

Getting out of the head and surrendering to the body's wisdom takes practice. Michael Chekhov gave the actor scales, just as the musician has scales. In undertaking these exercises we are aiming to find that moment when we realize that we are not dictating to the body, but allowing it to be our teacher.

This work is an act of inspiring the instrument into a state of availability. A musician doesn't perform with an instrument that is not tuned properly to a musical scale.

---

[1] *To the Actor*, 1.

Actors are those people who dare to step onto a stage and pretend to be someone else: living someone else's life, someone else's relationship, circumstances or situation. Actors should be worthy of this task. How do we become worthy? We have a responsibility to hone our instrument to the best of our ability. This task may represent a lifetime of effort. Our instrument is our humanity – our physical body – not a paintbrush or a pencil. Our work is about training ourselves to make ourselves worthy of being on a stage.

Unlike musicians, we actors live in our instruments. We take them wherever we go. Everything in our society wishes to destroy that relationship. Everything in our culture is more about our connection to external things: our devices, our machines. In our daily life, we are mostly unaware of our physical selves, except, perhaps, when we are in pain. By contrast, a class with Fern and Ted begins with asking the actors to take the time to be with themselves: to be awake and keenly aware of their own physical presence. Actors ask themselves about the condition of the material they will be working with today – what's happening in their physical body? They need to find the truth of their outer form while, at the same time, awakening their inner space.

We aim to re-educate ourselves, to develop a strong bodily awareness, to build what Chekhov calls 'a sensitive membrane, a kind of receiver and conveyer of the subtlest images, feelings, emotions and will impulses'.[2]

Fern says:

> We only have this body. That's what we are here to discover with this work. How the body and the imagination play together. How the inner and the outer speak to each other. We can't sit in our room and write, paint, or play a musical instrument. We only have this body. There is wisdom in the body.
> It is unfathomable. It's incomprehensible, and that is what we will spend this time together discovering. We are likely to be mystified, frustrated, because it seems inaccessible. There will be

---

[2] *To the Actor*, 2.

times when you will resist, or you can't be present – that's called being human.

Why do we do the exercises over and over? Sometimes an experience is there; sometimes it isn't. You keep seeking a connection between your inner and outer being. The inner and outer are in constant interplay.

As actors, we are the luckiest people in the world, because we can continue to examine the human condition and be fascinated by it. This way of working has different inroads. Maybe we find it, perhaps we don't, but we can and will have moments of discovering what is living in each of us. We can honor it and be grateful that it's there. Then you can use it as an artist.

Images

In *To the Actor*, Chekhov says that using our imagination effectively is a way to free ourselves of inhibitions.[3] The actor's life is built upon an active imagination: actors play freely with images, allowing images to live within them and influence them. The more specific an image is, the more potential it has to open otherwise hidden channels of expression. Often, images can give life to a character that would otherwise have been inaccessible.

Chekhov suggests that we put images on like articles of clothing. We allow the image to play the physical body. This requires us to get out of the way, surrendering our need to control the image. Instead, we allow the body to listen and inform us how the image wishes to manifest itself. We allow the images to play the body, our instrument.

Chekhov also suggests reading a script repeatedly and considering as you do so what is arising within you as an image, an imagination, an inner response.[4] Alternatively, sit with a partner and listen as *they* read your lines. Does an image come? The image might be something you have to cultivate. Listen a second time and see if movement is invited. Listen to find a space where you can dwell with your character, finding out how they look, how they move,

---

[3] *To the Actor*, 21–34.
[4] *To the Actor*, 21–34.

what they may treasure and how the space that they have chosen to inhabit seems. In other words, find your way towards your character not through thought alone but through an image that you allow to physically guide you.

You may want to sit and close your eyes and let an image of the character you are working on appear. Accept whatever image arrives. Then get up on your feet and climb into that image. Return from time to time to the inner vision, and let the image inform and enrich your work.

Work with fairy tales. Read a story slowly and ask questions of yourself as you go. Did you have an image of the door? The castle? The wicked creature? If you hold that image in mind when you talk about the door, the castle, the creature, the moment will come alive.

Another worthwhile exercise is to close your eyes and imagine somebody. Get up on your feet and embody the image of that person. Make big choices and fill those choices. You may notice you feel safer because it's your image making those choices. Trust that.

Fern says, 'Specificity of image cannot be stressed enough'. If you are telling a story, you are not just saying words: those words need to be wrapped around an image.

An image may create an atmosphere, or the atmosphere may evoke an image. Likewise, both image and atmosphere can awaken the life of gesture. An image is not necessarily visual. It may be a sensation, a sense of something, an intuition.

Tangible and intangible

The slow movement of an arm is tangible; we see it. The sensations that arise as a result are intangible.

In *To the Actor*, Chekhov says that the interplay of tangible and intangible is the simplest technical means for kindling your feelings.[5] Another way of thinking about this dichotomy is in terms of the visible and the invisible. The invisible changes the visible. The visible, done consciously, can change the invisible.

We can only get to the intangible through the tangible. All of the intangibles are awakened through the tangibility of the body. The

---

[5] *To the Actor*, 59.

intangible is as valuable as the tangible, and there is always this interplay between them.

Fern says, 'What we're always seeking is "what is the intangible here? What is the invisible here? And it's all waking up. "What are we waking up?"'

Sensing and thinking

Sensing is the key to the Chekhov work. Sensing is listening on a deeper level; listening that helps us make decisions. Sensing helps us know which road to take, lending authenticity to our choices.

You can either think about a character or you can sense something about that character. You might say you think the character's centre is in the head or in the chest. That's a very different thing than sensing. When you're sensing, you might say, 'it's my sense that they are not going to like that'. Sensing happens in the body.

When we are starting to discover who our character is, we apply different tools, using different parts of our body, until something lands that feels right. We give ourselves the opportunity to play and to explore: to find the seat of the character in our bodies.

Sensing is not intellectual but experiential.

The inspired state

The Chekhov work is about inspiring our instrument – the body – into a state of availability.

Our sources of inspiration are varied and often surprising. We can do the work, be as prepared as we possibly can be, and then meet with something unexpected; something that plays us, rather than being played *by* us. This doesn't mean that we are out of control; we are conscious every moment. When we have done the work and feel like *we* are being played, we have achieved the inspired state.

At this point, another part of our being – call it the 'higher I', the unconscious part of ourselves – begins to take over. Nobody can tell us where it comes from. In this state, we are taken over by our creative individuality. It brings us right into the present moment.

The inspired state is a foundation. Incorporating it into your being is an ongoing process of educating your instrument, opening yourself up to your own humanity. The Chekhov work gives us tools to find how we can inhabit the fullness of what is available to us in our humanity. In this way, we develop a participating consciousness in our actor's instrument, the body.

Ted says:

> The body is a world of movement: heartbeat, breath, circulation, all of which accelerate or decrease according to human emotion. We fly, we mould, we radiate. For many actors, words become their primary means of communication. Whereas with Chekhov's approach, the inner and outer become our primary source: inner gesture, qualities of movement, radiating and receiving all communicate to our fellow actors and the audience the story itself.

This is what Chekhov meant when he said, 'the actor is the theatre'.[6] In the Chekhov work, the emotion doesn't give rise to the gesture; the gesture gives rise to the emotion. We raise our shoulders in a questioning gesture, we straighten our spine in indignation, we stiffen in anger. We inhabit the body consciously and fully.

Crossing the threshold

Now we have discussed our key terms, we can embark on our journey. We are about to cross the threshold – that delicious moment in which the actor leaves their everyday life behind and commits to their work.

The remainder of this part will introduce you to the essentials of the Chekhov work.

This part (like the next, 'Transformative Tools') is designed for you to use alongside Part 5, 'Class Exercises'. You can read about each tool here, and then find the corresponding exercises in Part 5 to practice.

---

[6]Michael Chekhov, 'Open Lecture to Actors Held at "Actors Service", New York', 29 January 1942, https://collections.uwindsor.ca/chekhov/item/1084.

Expanding and contracting

The idea of expanding and contracting is an underpinning foundation for developing our psycho-physical relationship. You can introduce the whole aspect of psycho-physical through expanding and contracting; it's very available to any actor. Expanding and contracting are one of the most immediate tools in reaching our feeling life.

Expanding and contracting happen involuntarily in our everyday lives. When you walk out the door and it's the first beautiful day of spring, you expand. When someone is about to tell you something, and you can feel it isn't going to be good news, you begin to shrink or contract. Another example comes from the classroom. Imagine that the teacher has asked a question, and you have an excellent understanding of the answer. You want to be called on. Your whole being is occupying the space: you expand, and the teacher can't help but see and call upon you. Conversely, imagine you have no idea what the answer is. You think, 'please don't call on me', and you want to disappear. You contract. You diminish. You take away any spatial relationship.

How much of the space do you take up if you expand? How much space do you lose if you contract? The action will tell you something about your inner state. Listen to the movement itself. Become one with the movement, trusting that it will take you somewhere inwardly. There is a whole spectrum of experience between expanding and contracting. It's the journey of movement itself.

We can weave expanding and contracting into the fabric of the story we are telling or the character we are playing. It's beneficial to think about expanding and contracting in those moments in a play when you are receiving news, happy or sad. It can be useful to apply the concept in ensemble work: all of the actors might expand or contract as a particular event occurs. There is nothing particularly interesting in being expand*ed* or contract*ed*. It's the process of expand*ing* and contract*ing* as an activity that brings us into the present.

You may initially think of expanding as a joyous experience and contracting as a fearful or sorrowful experience. In truth, expansion

FIGURE 1 *Contraction, 2016. By Val Kissel*

can be a response to an experience of fear or alarm. There is a vast spectrum to both.

At the original Michael Chekhov Studio, the teachers who had worked with Chekhov himself at Dartington Hall and Ridgefield, Connecticut, taught expanding and contracting in the form Chekhov sets out in *To the Actor*. In this exercise, students would start from an expanded position and then go down on one knee, into a contracted position. They would then rise out into an expanded position and sink down again in a contracted position. Students would stay a long time in the final position, the contraction, strengthening that contracted state.

In the eighties, Ted began to discuss how powerful the idea of expand*ing* and contract*ing* was in playing a scene or fulfilling an event within a play. Contracting can be a release of something you are holding on to, or even a moment of self-protection or safety.

Expanding and contracting don't necessarily equate with opening and closing. The two are different processes. You can be expanded

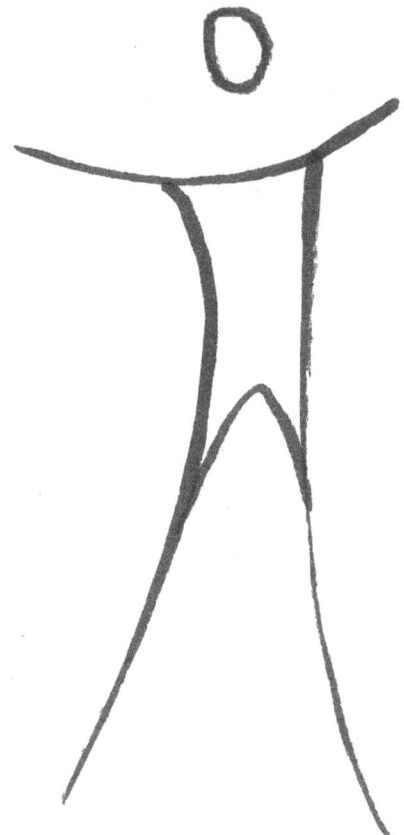

FIGURE 2 *Expanding, 2016. By Val Kissel*

and closed; you can be contracted and open. The dichotomy between expanding and contracting is related to your relationship with outer space; opening and closing is related to your relationship with inner space.

The movement between expanding and contracting can itself be filled with sensation, image, memory and emotion.

Try not to only use expanding as a yes and contracting as a no. Realize that expanding can be the no and contracting the yes. Try to resist limitations; open yourself up to what might be.

The movement will do the acting for you; that is the fun of it. As actors, we are always seeking to be played by the possibilities, in that inspired state. We are seeking a living process.[7]

The actor's ideal centre

The actor's ideal centre is a centre of warmth and light in the chest. We express ourselves with our belly or our head. We go out into the world through the centre in the chest. This is a starting point. The face reflects what the heart feels. Our arms and hands, of course, come out of that middle section. A lot of vital emotional expression is carried from the chest into the arms and hands. The ideal centre is where we meet the world.

As actors, we have to be present with what is happening within our bodies. We have to listen, notice and be aware of the ideal centre. This work grows through practice, and it's not to be forced. It grows as we continue to apply ourselves. We can only extend an invitation to enliven the ideal centre, and then rest easy within it.

This talk about being open – being available, allowing ourselves to be surprised, allowing ourselves not to be within what we know – implies vulnerability. But that's not necessarily so. We are working with the body, and the body gives us a foundation: the substance of our humanity.

In engaging with the Chekhov work, we are not trying to crack people open. We are aiming for a steadiness, a confidence that can also be described as a fullness of being, a fullness of self. You always have the freedom to explore, investigate, question and not know. Vulnerability is a huge aspect of being an artist, but walking out on unknown ground is its antidote – its remedy.

The invitation to open your ideal centre is a gentle invitation to find a place in the body where you can rest and feel at home within the essence of your being.

The ideal centre is a source of energy, where impulse and gesture may be born. It is up to each actor to consciously find their connection to that centre and continue deepening the connection.

---

[7]The Expanding and Contracting Class for Beginners with Ted is on page 90. The Advanced Class, page 92. Once you have tried those classes you may wish to explore with Fern, Opening and Closing, or Expanding and Contracting on page 93.

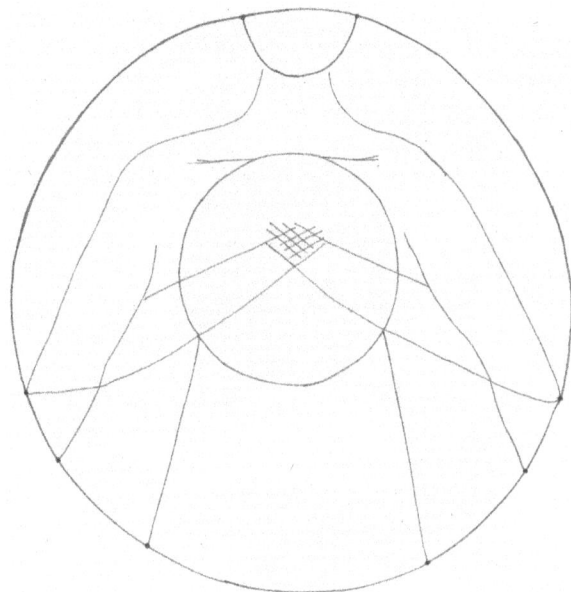

FIGURE 3 *The Actor's Ideal Centre, 2016. By Val Kissel*

Trouble arises when a demand is placed upon that centre to open, without the whole of an actor's being available as a support.

Working with the centre in the chest can open you in surprising ways, into something you didn't know was possible. This vulnerability without support – without a technique – can be destructive. However, the ideal centre is the centre of your being, so in working with it, you come to an essence within yourself. It's a place, an activity, a source of energy, but it's within your being. You are not at the mercy of your personality.[8]

The qualities of movement

The qualities of movement Fern and Ted talk about within the Chekhov work are moulding, floating, flying and radiating. (Some

---

[8] The Three Centres Class with Ted is on page 108.

Chekhov practitioners use the term 'flowing' for 'floating'. Choose the language that works best for you.) These relate to the four elements of earth, water, air and fire respectively. Like expanding and contracting, qualities of movement are essential for developing our psycho-physical relationship.

Qualities of movement are great training tools. They engage the whole aspect of the psycho-physical relationship: our full body, the space and our imagination. However, they are not just limited to training; qualities of movement can be useful in ensemble work. Qualities of movement can help us create and develop a character, explore a text or find the style of a particular play. They can heighten a moment in the play or add a quality to a gesture. At a certain place in a story, when something major has just taken place, any one of the four qualities of movement might carry the story further. At some points, qualities of movement influence the atmosphere.

We need to take care to keep our qualities of movement psycho-physical. If a movement is only physical movement, we are not genuinely allowing ourselves to participate fully; allowing the movement to play back on our inner life. There is no result in this work without the inner and the outer participating together.

A note on terminology: 'radiating'

Before we move forward, we need to address the different ways in which we use the word 'radiating' in the Chekhov work. We talk of radiating as a quality of movement, and we also talk of 'radiating and receiving' as a separate essential component of the work. When we talk of radiation as a quality of movement, we are talking about just that: movement, without any direction or gesture. The quality of movement that is radiating is about moving with the quality of fire, or with the quality of light.

Transitions between the qualities of movement and moments of change

Do not ignore the transitions between the qualities of movement. There are endless possibilities in moving from one quality of movement to the other: for example, from moulding to floating or from floating to flying. There is juice in the transition; there is discovery in the transition. An actor or a director can use these transitions to highlight dramatic moments and changes within a play.

Qualities of movement can be a great tool for approaching moments of change within a play: when the character becomes somebody else, or fails in a particular aspect to remain heroic.

In recent years, Ted and Fern have found that it can be helpful to harness fear or caution when applying moulding, floating and flying. Fear or caution heighten a moment or a circumstance: moulding fear, flying fear or floating fear.

Qualities of movement can inform gesture, as well. You can mould a gesture, float a gesture, fly a gesture or radiate a gesture. You can stay with one of these qualities and allow others to attach themselves to it and fill it out, keeping your focus on your original intention.

Qualities of movement and parts of the body

The specific parts of the body that resonate with each quality of movement depend on the individual actor.

In terms of moulding, you could mould with the chin, but lower parts, under the neck, may be more powerfully affected by moulding. When you are using moulding as your tool, be solidly in the lower half of your body. Plant your feet; allow your legs to be strong. Feel that the lower half of your body is available and that you are fully supported. You can apply moulding to the way you walk. Or look at your open hand, where it joins the wrists. That meaty, fleshy part of the hand has often been related to the will, the fingertips to thinking and the middle of the hand (the open palm, which can be very sensitive) to feeling. You can get quickly into moulding by working with that fleshy part of the hand.

When you are using floating as a tool, your head as it sits on your neck could help. We often get quickly into floating just by keeping the activity between the arms and torso. You may find that, when you lift your elbows a bit, you're floating. (You may feel that your arms lift in and of themselves). When you're floating, allow your feet to not be placed so solidly on the ground. Instead, feel water underneath your feet; allow yourself to get a sense of being carried.

When you're working with the quality of movement that is flying, you might feel as if someone has their hand on the small of your back, to lift you up into the air.

When you're radiating, it may help to imagine that there is light streaming through your fingertips.

When you are applying qualities of movement, it is vital that you are inwardly participating with your movement at every moment: as engaged inwardly as you are outwardly. The inner engagement will absorb tension, and enable you to refrain from seeking a result.[9]

Chekhov himself said:

After many years of trying to find this technique I found that everything we need in order to develop such a technique is already there in us, if we are born as actors. That means that we have only to find out which sides of our own nature have to be stressed, underlined, exercised, and the whole technique will be there.[10]

The four brothers

Chekhov talks about every work of art having four qualities, which he called 'the four brothers': ease, form, beauty and a feeling of the whole.[11]

As actors, we incorporate these four brothers into our creative process. An actor can develop a love affair with these four brothers because there are so many different ways to approach them.

It is worth seeking to emphasize sensation throughout your exploration of the four brothers.

Ease

Ease is the basic foundation of the Chekhov work. We can always go to another level of ease, regardless of how often we have practised. Chekhov suggests that an artist must always use lightness and ease as a means of expression.[12]

---

[9] QOM – A Beginner's Class with Fern is on page 95. The Advanced Class, page 99.
[10] Michael Chekhov, 'Michael Chekhov's First Class for Professional Actors', 7 November 1941, https://collections.uwindsor.ca/files/original/c05e92ea6e8514c94bfdbd2e4903b58efae0f482.pdf.
[11] *To the Actor*, 13.
[12] *To the Actor*, 13–14.

Ease is participating with your whole being in moving free of tension, free of ambition, free of effort. Ease is pleasurable. The ease we seek is not only in the physical body but in the inner being: being easy with yourself, easy with the day's tasks, easy in the body, easy in your approach to ease. An actor can bring ease into the most intense, violent situations and know that however strong the intention is, or the gesture is, they can do it with ease.

Form

Form is a living entity. It can relate to the physical body; the way an actor works with a chair, for example; the architecture of the space the actors are in; connections with fellow actors; or forms created with a whole ensemble. Our form speaks for us. Allow yourself to wake up to the way form feeds and nourishes the creative process. Start by looking at the form of your hand. Stay with the form, and become conscious of the form of the whole of the physical body, and each of its parts. What forms can your body create?

Beauty

The third brother, beauty, is difficult. Beauty, as a principle, does not mean that the actor has to be beautiful. Rather, beauty is in play when ease and form come together.

Over the years, Fern and Ted have approached this intangible feeling of beauty from many angles. For example, how do you handle a chair when you endow it with a quality of beauty: being valuable, precious, one of a kind? Does it have more significance than it had before? Similarly, hold an imaginary crystal in your hands. Allow yourself to feel the beauty of that imagined crystal, then hand it to another. Cultivate a sense of beauty in that transaction.

In working with beauty, we seek to find something of beauty and allow ourselves to discover how it affects our movement, our inner life.

Chekhov talks in *To the Actor* about how we must fill our lives with beauty.[13] Think about what it is that makes something beautiful.

---

[13]*To the Actor*, 16.

A feeling of the whole

And now we get to the last brother, a feeling of the whole. Chekhov talks about having the end of the play in you at the beginning of the play.[14] In cultivating a feeling of the whole, we are cultivating a sense of the wholeness of the play.

A harmonious blend of ease, form and beauty will ultimately develop on its own into a feeling of a well-integrated whole. It may result in a robust inward experience of this instrument of ours becoming, as Chekhov suggests, a 'piece of art within itself'.[15]

The four brothers together: bring your unknowing into being

It's easy to get into our habit body and feel that we know what ease, form and beauty are. But that takes us out of the present. Instead, we need to focus on the present moment: we need to allow ourselves to go beyond what we know, to discover what is beyond that. We need to work on bringing our unknowing into being; on being willing to say, 'I don't know the limits of this' or 'What I know is limited'.

If the four brothers feel elusive, imagine viewing a performance that is without ease, form or beauty. Activity is the essence and part of the joy of the Chekhov work. Chekhov says, 'relaxed in body – but active in spirit – the spirit must never be weak. An active spirit is part of our technical equipment – it must always be there'.[16]

The practice of these four brothers will permeate the body, making it more sensitive, noble and flexible.

The separate tools we choose to create a character must ultimately be infused into a well-integrated whole, resulting in a more harmonious and powerful performance. How can we do that? We can apply the four brothers. The four brothers' exercises in this book, practised assiduously, can help you develop a capacity

---

[14]*To the Actor*, 17–19.
[15]*To the Actor*, 13.
[16]Michael Chekhov, Exercises for Increasing Actor's Abilities: Significance; Activity and Ease, Form, Beauty; The Character's Inner Fire', 20 January 1938, https://collections.uwindsor.ca/chekhov/item/805.

for blending those separate elements harmoniously into an all-embracing entirety.[17]

Radiating and receiving

We explore radiating and receiving together. Both radiating and receiving become more evident when you find their polarity: receiving becomes fuller if you explore radiating; radiating becomes fuller if you explore receiving. One informs the other.

Radiating

When you radiate, your attention goes out and your interest goes out. Something moves out from you into the space. Radiating is an activity that engages the whole of the psycho-physical being, the inner and outer. When we are talking about radiation, we are talking about the life force within us.

In class, Ted and Fern employ the gesture of giving to awaken our capacity to radiate. You can participate in radiation with your whole being, putting the gesture into the space and getting a sense of what it feels like to radiate.

When you send out (radiate) a gesture, it will continue to move, and you can continue to move with it, following it. For example, when you throw a ball, you can follow it, using the ball to explore the fundamentals of radiation. If, as you throw the ball around a circle in a group of actors, you stay engaged, continuing to send the movement of the gesture, you are radiating. It's the movement that continues beyond the end of the physical gesture itself.

On a rehearsal room floor, when we are with a character, text, partner and situation, we are not in isolation. But in a classroom, and on these pages, our task is to isolate the activity of radiation, to find out what it actually is and to explore all its facets.

When we think of the word 'radiating', we often think of light or heat (as when we talked of radiating in the context of the qualities of

---

[17]Four Brothers - A Beginner's Class with Ted, is on page 100. Advanced Class, page 102.

movement, above). The word has a certain activity to it. Something releases; something pours out of us. It has to do with presence. To truly radiate, we have to be fully present.

The most human place from which to radiate is the ideal centre. If that centre is filled with light and warmth, the light gives of itself. You can activate radiating through gesture, touch, impulse and want. You can work alone to practise that.

You can explore radiation with a ball, then you can explore radiating to just a person.

Certain gestures can activate radiation involuntarily. If you are sitting in a café by yourself and see someone who you are very close to that you haven't seen for a long time, you might stand up involuntarily and feel your arms stretch out. 'Oh my God', you might say, 'I haven't seen you in over a year!' That activity of radiating comes naturally.

Giving our attention can also be a form of radiating. People radiate in the presence of a baby or a puppy. People radiate because of what is being drawn from them by the presence of the person that they haven't seen for a long time, the baby or the puppy.

Receiving

As we did with radiating, we seek to identify receiving as a separate activity and to explore our ability to isolate it and engage with it.

Receiving helps lay the foundation for developing our psycho-physical relationship. We receive in our everyday life when we take something in: we receive a sensation, an impulse, an image, a situation, another person or other people. Receiving requires an openness, a presence, an availability. We allow whatever is there to come to us, to affect us.

Receiving is more active than just listening; it is more participatory. We do listen with the whole body, not just the head. The wholeness of the body is required for all attempts to be available and open to truly listen.

Listen to a story being read, and then practise *receiving* that same story. They are two different experiences.

Receiving can also involve what we see. In receiving, we ask ourselves not just what another person is saying but also what they are trying to do. What response do they want from us? Receiving can also take us into the space that is not knowing. Making yourself available to receive means making yourself available to what is coming towards you. You're more open to allowing something to come to you and move through you if you are open, and open to your back-space.

Try not to get stuck in the act of just receiving into your body. Allow yourself to open into the back-space, and receive into that. We receive out of the back-space in our daily life. For example, when you're walking down the street late at night and hear a noise behind you.

Chekhov asks us to make what we do on a subconscious level conscious. Every aspect of the work entails a human process. Rather than inventing something new, Chekhov's work was to draw our attention to elements that have always been there: the emotional and spiritual parts of our humanity. As students, when we participate in an exercise encouraging us to expand or contract the physical body, or to radiate or receive, we find the exercise familiar because it's human. The tools associated with the Chekhov work are not a bag of tricks. They are part of you; part of your humanity.

The Chekhov work requires us to be open, available and receptive. This is the essence of receiving.

Again, a ball helps us to engage with the activity of receiving. By simply catching a ball, we are receiving, taking in what comes our way.

A person receiving a ball can consciously awaken the inner activity of taking in – receiving a ball in the same way they might receive a silent gesture from another person. Breathing in an event or an offering into the back-space is a shared experience that is mostly unconscious in our daily life. In our practice, we're simply making conscious those unconscious experiences that any physical activity encompasses.

Radiating and receiving together

The more you work with radiation and receiving – the more you work to isolate them – the more they become tangible. You can't do either of these activities without engaging the fullness of your being. There are moments, too, when receiving and radiating become one.

Throwing a ball to understand radiating and receiving

The ball provides a blueprint for our work as actors: to throw the ball is to give – to radiate – and to catch the ball is to take in – to receive.

We radiate intentions; we receive what other people are trying to do to us. We experience this as actors when we're in a circle, throwing a ball. Everyone is engaged, and there's a certain generosity to the activity. As we throw the ball, something occurs physically: the little lines of tension resting on the body's surface are released. In Fern and Ted's classes, the class throws the ball underhand. It's a very gentle way to give the ball, so that everyone can feel comfortable with the activity. The experience of making that underhanded throw should embody the word 'give'. The act of scooping from behind and giving out the ball can feel very generous. It's a kind of release. The ball leaves your hand and goes out somewhere into space.

Throwing the ball illustrates the primary activity of an actor: to give and receive, to make contact with another. As the ball travels around the room, the space is filled with both the outer and the inner activity.

In this activity, the physical object, that is, the ball, grounds the student. There is nothing abstract about it. When this object leaves a hand and goes out into space, it can begin to awaken sensation, an inner activity. There is a moment before we throw the ball to someone in which we simply contact them.

As you throw, let go of any need to be social, to smile or to be pleasant. Simply connect with another person who is looking back at you. Make sure they are in readiness to receive the throw. Let the body calculate the distance between you. The next thing that occurs is an impulse from within that is a stream that moves out from you. It's on that stream that you throw the ball.

You can spend weeks finding out how to release and receive the ball: finding how to be in the body and experience movement and the pleasure that can be gained in this way. Ted's and Fern's ball exercises appeal to our sense of play, free of judgement. They are emphasizing ease and letting go of undue effort. They offer an invitation to us to be curious, to explore, to investigate and to free ourselves of goals that have to be attained.

Throwing the ball – practising conscious giving and receiving – is a good foundation for almost any aspect of the Chekhov work.

FIGURE 4 *Ted Pugh, 2018. Photography by Jessica Maynard*

The technique of radiating and receiving

All the elements of the Chekhov work are activities we do every day, unconsciously and involuntarily. We are constantly gesturing towards something, opening, closing, receiving or radiating. When we engage in the exercises set out in this book, we are making the unconscious conscious.

You might find that sometimes, when you are doing an exercise, you desire more than what you are experiencing. In this situation, you may be asking something of your instrument that it does not want to do. It does not want to be forced or pushed. It is telling you, 'that's all I can do at this moment'.

It's important to let radiating begin and end naturally, without forcing it. Otherwise, you are controlling the process in the wrong way. When radiation has its time and ends, something else begins to happen.[18]

The three physical centres – thinking, feeling and will

In terms of the Chekhov work, a centre is a source of inner activity and power within your body that effects a psychological change, or from which impulses for movement originate.

In the Chekhov work, the three physical centres are:

- the head centre (thinking)
- the chest centre (feeling)
- the stomach centre (will)

Warming up our three physical centres is one way we can prepare the body for the Chekhov work. Ted and Fern always begin their classes with awareness exercises, regardless of what the ultimate goal of the class is. They start with where the actor is and what they have available to them.

In life, almost all of us are pretty unconscious below the chin. We need to slow down, find ourselves emotionally and physically and try to embrace this awareness. We can slowly get rid of our sense of resistance and move to a greater sense of openness and ease.

We work with the centre in the head for clarity, the centre in the chest for opening and the centre in the stomach for strength and vitality. Warming up these three centres is essential; in this way, we are full-bodied when we start applying the essential and transformative tools. These three physical centres make us whole. They allow us to play our bodies and bend them to our will.

It should be pointed out that we already acknowledge these centres in our everyday life, and through our language. We say things like, 'When she told me that, my heart sank'. Or, 'He popped into my head'. Or, 'She's got guts'.

Chekhov discussed the ideal centre in detail.[19] Ted was taught about the ideal centre by the Dartington ladies in the early 1980s

---

[18]Radiating and Receiving Classes with Fern start on page 103.
[19]We have also discussed the Actors Ideal Centre on page 22-23

at the Michael Chekhov Studio. His understanding of the three centres as a group came from his work in Anthroposophy. In the late eighties, he brought these concepts into his teaching.

The Actors' Ensemble used to start with the ideal centre when warming up the three physical centres. Ted came to understand that it was more helpful for them to ground themselves first with the lower centre, followed by the head and lastly the chest. That's how warming up centres is now practised in most places.

To locate your physical centres, you need to have a good relationship with your physical body. If you feel any difficulty in locating a particular centre, put your hand on your belly and breathe from the centre you are having difficulty with: either the stomach, the chest or the head. Feel that your mouth and nose are taking in air from that particular area.

When working with actors who are coming to Chekhov for the first time, Fern and Ted always begin with physical centres. This tends to segue into other elements of the work.

A true embodiment of the three physical centres can help you approach the text itself, your voice itself, your speech itself. Working with the centres can awaken and enliven the text for you, so that it is constantly feeding into you and you are feeding in to it. Deciding which physical centre your character leads with could be one of the first doors you open in creating a character.

There are no rules. Play, investigate. Trust your body, your impulses and your creative individuality.

Chekhov says, 'you must have respect for your body as an instrument'.[20] Our amazing bodies are an unlimited resource we can tap into by connecting to the physical sources of our own energy. Working with our physical centres is one of the ways in which we can play our instruments.

In working with our physical centres, we need to always begin by sensing the condition in which we find our bodies on that particular day. What does your body have to say to you? Perhaps your will needs a little more attention today than it did yesterday? Stay open and available to what is happening in your physical centres. Ideally, the belly should be warm, the head clear and awake and the chest open.[21]

---

[20]Michael Chekhov, 'The Objective, the Aesthetic Conscience, the Actor's Body, Feeling of Ease', 14 December 1937: https://collections.uwindsor.ca/chekhov/item/762.
[21]The Three Centres' Class with Ted begins on page 108.

We can bring physical centres into our work with qualities of movement. For example, it helps to work with moulding by beginning in the belly: moulding grounds you and gets you down into the earthly elements. Floating could entail working high up, a little above the head; the sense of that centre lifts you, not out of the body but away from the earthly elements. When it comes to flying, you might like to imagine that your centre is in the collarbones, and that your collarbones are wings; in this way, you become free of the earth and enter into the element of air. When it comes to radiating, you might go right into the ideal centre, which you might imagine filled with warmth, light and fire.

Directions

This section on directions is largely indebted to the work of Ted's and Fern's colleague and dear friend Bethany Caputo, who teaches occasionally at the school in Hudson. Bethany developed the concept of directions after twenty years of doing the Chekhov work. She is now Artistic Director of Chekhov Studio NYC in NY.

Bethany's concept of directions was originally inspired by teacher Merry Conway. Its application and translation into Chekhov have developed over the years.

Like many of the Chekhov tools, the principle of directions is based not on any theory of acting but on the laws of the universe.

Bethany says:

There is the law of gravity. Science tells us solids, liquids and gases expand and contract. Utilising these facts, we can begin at the beginning of the psycho-physical experience. When you encounter an event, do you want to move away from it, towards it, do you grow bigger or smaller from it, do you rise out of it or sink from it? If you can sense this, and if your body can answer it for you, then you are on your way to sensing something more nuanced, like what the body wants to do as it moves outward, like to discover, to enlighten, to illuminate, to break open, etc. Direction is one of those fundamental first steps in any action. The directions are forward, backward, out, in, up and down.

Bethany believes our inner life is always in some kind of movement, and that movement almost always has a clear direction. You may not know the exact nature of that movement, but you can 'attune your awareness to at least detect the direction of that movement'.

When we are working with direction, we begin by awakening ourselves to what arises in us when we consciously move in one of six particular directions: forward, backward, out, in, up and down. What do we experience when we suggest to ourselves that we are only interested in what is in front of us? What do we experience when we suggest that our attention is only backward? We can ask similar questions for all six directions. 'It's essential that we don't act through this exercise', Bethany says. Rather, 'it is a kind of exploration of our own humanity'.

What arises in us if we choose to make one direction dominant for some time? Sometimes, what arises is a version of ourselves that is ambitious, or a version of ourselves that is deeply sad. A suggestion of character can appear, or of circumstance, but this begins with the self. Whatever transformation takes place comes from the undeniable experience of these universal truths: forward, back, out, in, up and down. As Bethany attests, 'Direction is psychophysical'.

We can think of direction in psycho-physical terms. The exercises on direction in Part 5 of this book are about experiencing the potential of the psychological value of direction. Our first step is to inhabit a sense of direction, so we can move into a sense of action.

Front-space and back-space

Although Chekhov himself didn't talk explicitly of directions, he did mention back-space; just not as part of any particular exercises. Bethany says, 'An awareness of front-space and back-space is an awareness of the direction of your energy and the psycho-physical properties that direction wakes up'. Simply put, front-space is about dialling up energy, and back-space is about dialling it down. To give an example, working on stage is more about front-space, and working on camera (depending on style and shot size) is more about back-space.

These concepts of front and back are already inherent in the way we conceptualize our experiences and speak of them. We talk, for example, about being 'on the front line' or 'on the back foot'.

In and out

In exploring the in and out directions, you could simply do Chekhov's exercise on expanding and contracting.[22] Bethany uses the concept of expanding and contracting in her teaching. Her 'Working with In' and 'Working with Out' exercises, which appear in Part 5, can be seen as a precursor to expanding and contracting. They can also be seen as related but different.

Bethany encourages you to think of these exercises in terms of introverted and extroverted – not the personality types, but as a direction for your attention. When you go in, it's because your attention is drawn inwards. When you go out, it's because your attention is pulled outward.

Bethany's exercises on working with directions are not meant to be the end of the line. Rather, they are the beginning of sensing the psycho-physical.

If you can sense yourself moving in a particular direction, you can sense the psychological value of that direction. You are then on your way to sensing more complex experiences, like gestures.

Direction is a fundamental first step. Do you want to go towards someone or away from them? Do you grow in the presence of a person, or do you shrink?

If you can sense the answers in your body, you are on your way to sensing something more nuanced, like what the body wants to do as it moves outward: perhaps to discover, to illuminate or to break open.

To explore directions is to explore a universal experience. Much like Chekhov's ideas about archetypes, directions express a kind of universal truth. Bethany refers to directions as one of the bold strokes of the psycho-physical experience. 'There is a world to explore in each direction: very simple but quite vast.'

Bethany says:

You cannot talk about movement and not speak of direction. However, in the twenty-six years I have taken classes full time, and with many Chekhov teachers, no one isolated directions and worked with them exclusively. Usually, it was an element of an exercise and not what the activity was centred around. About

---

[22]*To the Actor*, 5–6.

thirteen years ago, I took a workshop with Merry Conway, and she did a warm-up centred around directions. In all my years of studying the Chekhov technique, no one had isolated the experience of directions before. I had many experiences working with gestures and was encouraged to know in what direction a gesture began, but I had never taken a step back to focus on direction itself. It was a complete revelation to me. The workshop was focused on something else entirely; this exercise was just a warm-up. But I went home after that weekend and taught my very next class with an expanded version of what she had done and with a slightly different perspective. And since then, I have continued to develop it. In truth, I rarely begin a class without starting with directions. It gives us a language, a kind of lexicon that I continue to refer back to throughout a workshop and well beyond. It truly is a common language that everyone already knows; they just have to bring their awareness to it.

Throughout the years, Bethany has often worked in the back-space, which is a Chekhov approach. She had been guided many times to be aware of and use her back-space, to put an image in the back-space or to enhance her awareness of the back-space to increase her presence or size. This was the closest she came to an isolated use of directions in the Chekhov work as it was taught to her.

The concept of directions is an introduction to the psycho-physical experience and to the vast wisdom and simplicity of the body. It acknowledges the way the body communicates with us, informing us of what we feel or what activity we are involved in.

Directions have become, for Bethany, almost a separate element altogether. 'Independent but, of course, very much in the world, spirit and practice of Chekhov's psycho-physical technique.'

Bethany believes that the concept of directions is inherent to Chekhov's body of work. She has simply defined and isolated the concept.

Thinking about direction directly helps us to think about psychological gesture (see 'Transformative Tools' below for more information on psychological gesture). If you are in tune with what direction your body is going, you have taken your first step in the direction of the gesture that is living in you. Bethany says:

> If you know you are going forward, your body is telling you with all its cells that you are going forward, you know you are

heading towards a penetration or a push or a reach or any other gesture that is a forward-moving gesture. The direction is just the first step, but, as one of my former teachers, the late Lenard Petit, always said, 'Your body will never lie to you.'

To know the direction in which you are going is the first step. Then you can begin to craft and discover what activity you are involved with. Psychological gesture is a direct next step after exploring the truth of direction.

Directions and gesture

When you are beginning to craft a gesture, Bethany shares, let your first question be, 'What is the direction the body wants to go in after you say the words? For example, does the body want to push, pull or expand? This requires just one step. When our body is trained and we are sensitive to the way our bodies move directionally in space, the body will never lie to us in answering this question. That direction will be the truth of that gesture. It is a truth, and it can be trusted. Sense the direction of the gesture first, and the rest of the body will follow, forming a more fleshed-out, complex and nuanced action.'

For the purposes of discovery, try expanding in different directions. Expand up, down, forward or backward.

Try pulling from above and below, or pushing forward and backward. For example, Bethany suggests, 'Try to feel the subtle difference in the story when you push backward instead of forward. Push out, and push down as if to squelch an emotion that you do not want to reveal.'

How to use direction in developing a character

Direction can lead to character. Someone who is constantly moving forward may be quite ambitious. Or anxious. Or seeking. Directions can lead to activity, to sensation, to the atmosphere. Bethany says:

> It could be argued that New York City is a very front-space place. Things move at a rapid pace, and most of it is to gain ground, to

move forward in life. The collective consciousness of the town could be argued to be ambitious. Creating this atmosphere could be helped by creating a sense of forward movement into one's playing space.

Alternatively, direction can simply be a quiet knowledge or awareness. Sometimes our performances must be on a small scale – for example, in front of a camera – and sometimes we don't have much time to make a choice about a scene or a circumstance. Bethany says: 'To be aware of what direction you are going in, just the awareness of your inner experience of direction can be enough to guide your performance in the right direction.'

A Practical Application for Directions: The First Pass at a Script

For Bethany, applying the concept of directions can be a simple and accessible way to begin to tease out the meaning in a script. 'If you are at the stage when you know very little about a scene, in your first pass at the scene, simply ask yourself, do I want to go towards this other person or away from them?'

Bethany notes that a teacher might offer suggestions to actors as they first approach a scene, recommending that they concentrate on front-space or back-space, moment by moment. Putting themselves in a character's shoes, an actor might ask, 'Am I social with other characters, inclusive, or more reclusive and preoccupied with myself? Do I feel heavy, weighted down by something, or lighter, more carefree?' Answers to these questions will be informed by knowledge of front-space and back-space.

Trajectories

Bethany uses the 'Trajectories' exercise (see Part 5)[23] the most when coaching actors. It's about picking one trajectory (front and back, or in and out, for example) and exploring it. Bethany says,

---

[23]Page 90.

'It is terribly effective and can be easily layered without disturbing actors' choices for their text'.

Bethany brought this idea into rehearsals with Fern and Ted for their show *Washington Square*, working along the lines of up and forward, and conversely down and backward. (This invited in a diagonal direction.) There are limitless possibilities for working with directions in this way.

Because the idea of directions is a broad stroke – like, for example, the idea of tempo is – an actor can use the idea without it eclipsing action or any other particular element. As Bethany explains it, an awareness of directions moves the actor so immediately that it can fade into the background of our attention and still be working. 'In other words', Bethany says, 'it won't take up valuable real estate in your consciousness. It can also lead to more complex images or actions'. The idea of directions can guide a shift for a character as they evolve throughout the play.

Final points on directions

The idea of directions provides us with guiding questions; for example:

- 'Does this image/tempo/gesture launch me into the front-space? Or does it send me back into the back-space?'
- 'Does this image that I am working with make me heavier or lighter?'
- 'Does this gesture that I am working with take up a lot of space or very little?'
- 'When I work with a personal atmosphere of (for example) the colour yellow, do I go out from myself or go inwards?'

As you continue to work with directions, Bethany shares, focus on extending your awareness beyond what is generated in the body. Yes, engaging the body is the first step, but as you build your capacity for sensing direction, Bethany says, 'eventually you will be able to experience your supple and receptive body like honeycomb, and you will feel that energy can flow very easily through you in all directions.

You will become more aware of intrinsic shifts in direction, and then your work will be simply to follow those movements, rather than having to generate the experience extrinsically.'

In working to become aware of sensation and experience, we move grossly at first. Still, eventually, we can detect these things on a more nuanced level, and we find that we are following the movement of an inner life instead of creating it. In this way, Bethany says, 'we are in movement all the time, active inwardly, and yet free to be available outwardly to the present moment'.[24]

As Chekhov tells us, 'you will never fail to win this game unless your impatience hurries the results'.[25]

---

[24] The Directions Class with Bethany Caputo begins on page 110.
[25] *To the Actor*, 79–80.

Part 3

Transformative tools

Transformation, Chekhov tells, is what all actors long for.

The essentials set out in the previous part together comprise a foundation for developing the psycho-physical, which is the core concept of the Chekhov work. They are the fundamentals. This section, 'Transformative Tools', will take your practice further. This section will introduce you to some tools that will build on those essentials and take you deeper into the Chekhov work – and towards the transformation that is at the heart of acting itself.

This section, like the previous part, is designed for you to use alongside Part 5, which sets out exercises for the tools discussed.

The Chekhov work makes it possible for an actor to truly experience the body–mind connection and to allow the imagination to alter their physical, emotional and soul life. In coming to grips with the essentials of the previous part, we have learnt to trust the body and its movement to take us where we want to go inwardly. We have begun to understand how a movement can spark an image, a previously unencountered sensation, a sense of venturing into the unknown, or the unveiling of a soul experience hidden away within us, only now being brought to consciousness.

The Chekhov work gives us tools to uncover different aspects of our being, digging ever deeper, constantly expanding. The transformative tools set out in this section will allow us to build capacities that would otherwise remain unknown and thus unavailable.

This work should be joyful. It's about learning how to get out of the way so something else can happen. The work should be freeing; it should be about accepting our own creative individuality. This is a journey of discovery.

The transformative tools set out in this section are:

- imaginary centres
- staccato and legato
- inner and outer tempo
- quality and sensation
- atmosphere
- the imaginary body
- archetype
- psychological gesture

First, let's explore the transformative tool of imaginary centres.

Imaginary centres

We spoke in Part 2 of three physical centres – the head, the chest and the will centre. We are now expanding that idea to encompass imaginary centres: other places in the body from which a character might operate from. In using this idea, we are taking an image and using both our imagination and our physical body to embody that image. If we imagine that our impulses come from a particular location in the body, it can be almost as if our breathing, speech and movements all emerge from that place; that base.

The three physical centres we talked about in Part 2 can also be imaginary centres, in that we can use our imagination to give them various qualities. For example, the centre in the head could be light-filled, or it could have a small, dark, hard centre. The centre in the chest might feel high and warm, like the sun, or dark and foreboding or it might even feel empty, filled with longing.

When we incorporate an imaginary centre into our experience of the relationship between our physical and emotional body, we might find that we suddenly feel like someone else. This can be a delicious feeling.

Imaginary centres allow us to go to a place which is not ourselves. In working with an imaginary centre, we are seeking transformation.

Work with imaginary centres is experiential, in that it involves the body and mind, the body and soul, the body and the emotional life working together. It affects your whole being, including your psychological life. Imaginary centres enable you to remove a conception of yourself that is limited: they provide a doorway to riches in terms of character work.

'All our exercises', Chekhov said, 'are appealing to this thing: how to coax the feelings into our bodies'.[1]

Choosing your imaginary centre

How do you choose an imaginary centre? What is the guiding image? What is the starting point? The answers to these questions will come from reading and rereading a play, studying the character and listening to the images your reading and study suggest to you. You will find that an impulse will arise: an image of where you sense the centre is going to be. Take that image, put it in your body, then experience it. Try it out. Maybe it's small. Perhaps you haven't yet found the right size for it. Perhaps it has a movement, or perhaps it's static. Perhaps it has a colour. You won't yet know where the image will lead or what result it will have until you get up on your feet and experience it. Resist figuring it out beforehand. If you trust the availability of the image, the body will affect the voice and the voice the body.

Let's say you have figured out that a character's centre is in the pit of your stomach. Once you know this, give that centre a quality. Is it soft and warm, or heavy and hard?

Working with imaginary centres

Your imaginary centre might be a cold, upraised right eyebrow, or a light shining out of you from the top of the chest. It could be on the tip of your nose, slightly below your rear end, in your hands or in your eyes. It might be within somebody else, an entirely separate

---

[1]Michael Chekhov, 'Desire for Exercising Regularly; Characters; Future Theatre Plans; Fire – Flaming Feelings; Archetypal Feelings; Right Feelings through Right means; Eurythmy; Actor-director Relationship', 16 January 1938, https://collections.uwindsor.ca/files/original/0b09e77011a6688c0839f8c81be6c62207d6443d.pdf.

character. You might find your character has no centre and spends the duration of the play seeking it in various ways.

In introducing imaginary centres, Ted and Fern usually begin by asking the class to put specific images/sensations into their physical centres. For example, they might ask them to create a will centre with warm, runny honey, or an empty chest centre, or a head centre filled with ice. They then ask students to experiment with different locations within their bodies and with other images: razor blades in the eyes, a steel spine, a pencil nose. They explore what it feels like when our imaginary centre is within another person: a husband, a lover, a baby, a child, a puppy.

Fern and Ted ask students to explore how they approach everyday activities while exploring each imaginary centre: walking, sitting, having a drink of water, brushing their hair. First, students explore these centres fully physically, and then they move on to text. How does the imaginary centre affect the text?

In working with imaginary centres, we never cast any of our experiences in concrete or feel that we are tied to a particular choice. Sometimes, we'll make a choice and find that it isn't quite right. That's fine; if it doesn't work, choose something else. Explore, investigate and play with the imaginary centre as a living entity. Sometimes you have to make an extreme choice to awaken something in you as the character, and then pull it back. If you find that you are not managing to get beyond yourself, try a different part of the body.

You know that you have found your character's imaginary centre when you feel a sense of potency, of juiciness. If your choice doesn't take you anywhere – if it's not strong, robust, compelling – perhaps it's just a clever idea. If the imagination doesn't begin to transform you, if it doesn't start to percolate, then there is no point to it.

Moving and changing centres

Imaginary centres can move, and the actor will change if they follow the movement. Alternatively, the centre might stay in the same place but its quality might change. The most effective use of a moving centre is a particular text's moments of change. It can be a powerful moment when an actor stands on a stage and changes centres in front of the audience. In *Hamlet*, the new king rises from praying with the realization that, 'My words fly up, my thoughts remain below; words without thoughts never to heaven go'.[2] It is easy to imagine a moving centre at this moment in Claudius. In *Richard II*, the king's centre might move from his head (bound up with his identity with the crown's authority) to somewhere else, in the absence of the crown. To feel a centre sink or rise is to feel what a particular story is about at that moment. The movement of sinking or rising might advance the play.

A centre in the head might sink to the stomach, or a centre in the chest might rise above the head. A centre in the chest might move into the space immediately behind the actor: into the back-space. This might have the effect of suspicion or paranoia, or alternatively, a sense of spiritual support. A centre that is outside the character, in another character, might move over the course of the play into the initial character's chest: for example, upon the character's restoring their self-respect or coming to a greater understanding of the reality of their circumstances. An ever-moving centre could have the effect of indecision, confusion or even insanity. A centre above the head might suddenly begin bouncing up and down, lending a comic effect to an actor playing a clownish figure. When an actor feels the centre moving, they will do well to follow that movement consciously, allowing it to have its desired effect.

Change in a centre's quality can also mark significant moments of change. A bright, warm centre in the chest could become cold, dark or empty. There could be a change of colour, from light blue to fiery red. A low, warm centre could change into a fire or conversely a block of ice. The centre in the chest could be a candle flame growing into the sun or vice versa – a sun could diminish into a small candle flame. These changes might burst upon a character in a moment, or gradually change through a scene or over the course of the entire play.

As actors, we can become paralyzed by a director's suggestion that a specific moment should establish a total change in our character. Imaginary centres can come to our aid in our struggle to clarify those moments.[3]

---

[2] Shakespeare, *Hamlet*, act 3, scene 3.
[3] The Imaginary Centres Class with Fern is on page 117. Straight Line, Curves and Imaginary Centres with Ted, page 131.

Staccato and legato

Staccato and legato are musical terms to do with articulation; they are opposites. A 'staccato' notation requires a musician to play the notes as short, crisp and detached as possible; a 'legato' notation requires smooth, connected notes. In the context of the Chekhov work, staccato and legato are tools to awaken our awareness of space and direction. Working with staccato and legato requires us to release unnecessary tension, seek a fullness of body and focus on the whole aspect of sending out and sustaining. We have impulse, action, sustaining and preparation.

You can hear the qualities of staccato and legato in the words themselves. Staccato. Allow yourself to say it; get a sense of what it feels like in and around your mouth. The tempo of it. Now say 'legato', and again listen to its sound and tempo. The words themselves will carry you into the movements. It's fun to play with this.

Moments of change within a play can be highlighted by using staccato and legato. For example, in *A Midsummer Night's Dream*, when Titania faces Oberon in the 'forgeries of jealousy' speech,[4] an actor may choose to give parts of the speech a staccato quality. Conversely, the speech that comes directly after, when Titania is talking about the mother of the changeling boy ('his mother was a votress of my order') may be influenced by the quality of legato. So too may Titania's question when she wakes up to Bottom singing[5]: 'What angel wakes me from my flowery bed?' The musicality of the sentence lends itself to legato.

Staccato and legato aren't gestures but can add a quality to a gesture. If you are pushing in staccato, you have a very different intention than when you are pushing in legato.

Staccato and legato are invaluable as training tools when actors are developing a sense of the full body. Sometimes it's in exploring staccato and legato that actors have their first real experience of being full-bodied. Fern and Ted share that it takes time to develop staccato and legato. The actor needs to ask themselves; is something going out from you?

---

[4] Act 2, scene 1.
[5] Act 3, scene 1.

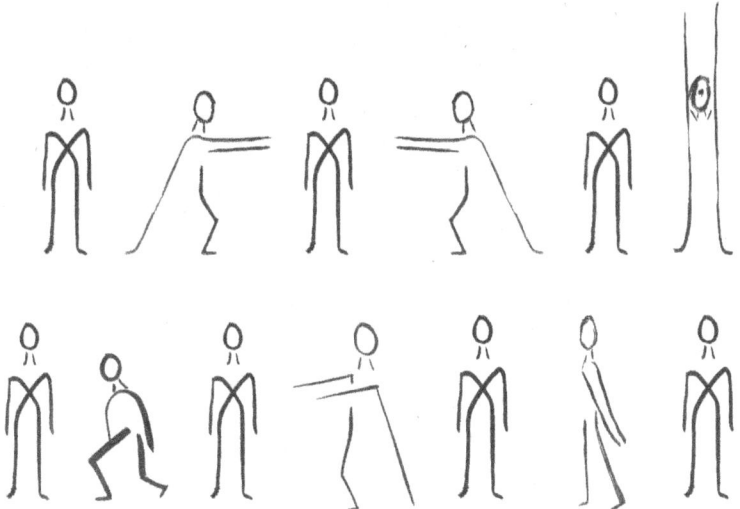

FIGURE 5 *Staccato and Legato, 2016. By Val Kissel*

The polarity of staccato and legato

We talked about polarity in the context of radiating and receiving above. Exploring the polarity of radiating and receiving enables you to understand each better. The same is true for staccato and legato. It is worth exploring the contrast between strong, short, quick, lightning, staccato movements and legato movements that flow like water. That which is awakened in the body is different in each case. Exploring this polarity can foster discoveries about character.

Using staccato and legato to fill out a character

Staccato and legato can be useful parameters when you are figuring out a character's temperament. A staccato temperament could be sanguine, quick and sometimes distracted. A legato temperament could be melancholic or phlegmatic. This aspect might be one of the last things you arrive at when you are figuring out a character. However, it could also be a good starting point. The choices are limitless, and there are no rules.

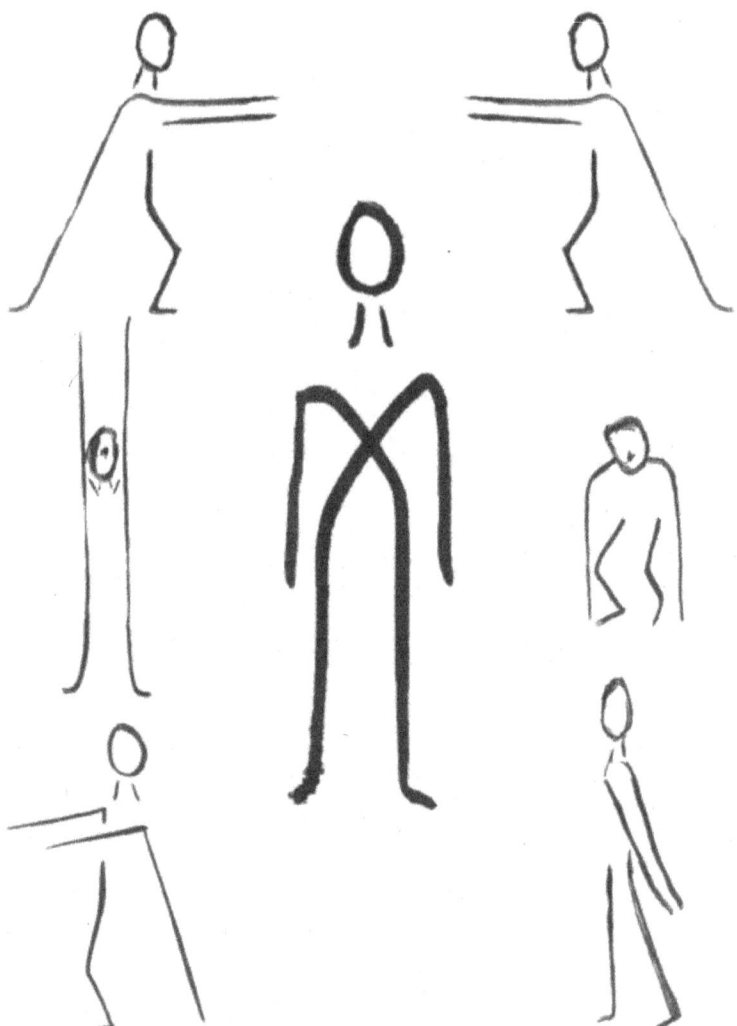

FIGURE 6 *Staccato and Legato II, 2016. By Val Kissel*

You might find your way into a character by listening intently to the musicality of staccato or the musicality of legato.[6]

---

[6]Staccato and Legato with Fern, page 96.

Inner and outer tempo

In the Chekhov work, tempo is seen as an inner reality that stimulates and gives rise to an emotional response. If it becomes external, it becomes behaviour; it becomes something that is explicitly indicated. This is not what we're looking for when we talk about tempo.

In our inner life, our inner world, tempo is emotion. An alarming event can trigger a rise in tempo, bringing us into an emotional state. To use *Hamlet* again as our example, when an actor playing Horatio sees the old king's ghost for the first time at the beginning of the play,[7] the tempo of their inner reality might increase, which would give rise to emotion. Increasing or decreasing the tempo allows the actor authentic emotional content.

Pace is an outer form of tempo. When a scene is dragging, a director might instruct us to pick up the pace, either vocally or in our physical movement. Thinking about tempo and pace as different aspects is useful too. A director might say, 'I want your character to start cleaning the house, just fiddling around in the kitchen, but I want you to get faster and faster and more frantic as the scene progresses'. Now, we can fulfil that direction physically, picking up the pace of our behaviour. But if you are able, picking up the inner tempo simultaneously could bring a hysterically funny – or alarming – aspect to the scene. If the inner tempo is alive, you are always connected to it. That gives you a strong base that you can plug into every night.

Inner and outer tempo are also one of the elements we use in building a psychological gesture, which is discussed below.

In their classes, Ted and Fern often use a metronome to explore tempo. If you don't have access to a metronome, staccato and legato (see previous pages) can provide helpful tools for working with inner and outer tempo. Alternatively, pose yourself some explorative questions. For example, what is it to move quickly and lightly? Embody those movements fully, and then take them into your inner reality.

Can you work with a staccato movement inwardly and engage in a legato movement outwardly? If you have fully embodied a fast-paced tempo, and it's living in you, your whole being will be

---

[7] Act 1, scene 1.

inwardly vibrating with that tempo. Still, outwardly, everything is fluid; everything is legato. You've given yourself an experience of polarity – the inner and the outer.

Alternatively, your whole being, both the inner and outer, might be in line with the ticking of the metronome. Similarly, your whole being may be either legato or staccato, both inwardly and outwardly.[8]

Quality and sensation

When a physical action is completed with consciousness, a reaction or echo follows: an emotional response – a sensation – that the movement has awakened. The movement is the physical body and the sensation is the soul: the psycho-physical.

Opening ourselves up to sensation, our feeling life, is the quickest pathway to our feelings. What we are trying to do is to close that gap between impulse, gesture and sensation, to the point that it all becomes one thing. If you can achieve this, you are more alive, more expressive. When a new impulse or sensation comes, you listen to it. You acknowledge it, and you use it.

If there is no sensation, then the actor is either not awake enough to acknowledge what is happening within, or they are in their head and thinking their way in, rather than feeling. In this case the sensation may be a whisper – something the actor is not willing to acknowledge because they don't think it is strong enough, or judge that it isn't the correct response. To remedy this, the actor needs to find what it is not to be divided: to be totally participating, to be one with whatever the movement is. This takes an enormous amount of concentration and focus.

Quality and sensation are transformative tools that together provide another pathway to our feeling life. Chekhov tells us that an actor moves with a quality and is met with a sensation.[9] He gives the example of raising the arm with the quality of caution, which will bring the actor to the sensation of caution.

Fern and Ted believe the danger in working with quality and sensation is in trusting your habitual body. For example, once you

---

[8]QOM and Tempo Class with Ted is on page 124. Sensation and Tempo with Ted, page 126.
[9]*To the Actor*, 58.

receive a suggestion to move with a quality of sadness, you might say, 'Oh, I know what it is to be sad'. Then when you start moving, you may find that you are moving with your memory of what you think sadness is. Fern and Ted tend to avoid working with the qualities of joy, sadness and anger at the beginning of their work with students on quality and sensations, because the temptation for actors is to go to these habitual responses, which leaves little room for being open to discovery.

In the Chekhov work, we are seeking that place where you surrender yourself to moving with a particular quality: where you participate in the seeking fully, so that you are not divided from yourself. The movement is at one with the quality, and you seek and trust that the quality will be met with a feeling: a sensation and a bodily sense of it. As you work with quality and sensation, engage with moving with the quality without worrying about whether the sensation is there or not. Surrender to engaging in the activity, staying with the quality you have chosen. It can be power, heat, fire or gentleness. It can be a colour. The truthfulness and authenticity of the movement are what will bring about a true sensation.

Large packages of feelings/sensations and our personal feelings

Chekhov talks about large packages of feelings/sensations in comparison with our personal feelings.[10] Our personal feelings limit us. If we approach what we don't know, we may discover elements of a feeling – joy, for example – that we didn't know existed. There is more to joy, anger and love than we personally experience. We can access these big packages with practice.

In coming to the Chekhov work, you come into your feeling life, but in a different way to what you might expect. You are not invested in it personally, because the feeling life opens to you through imagination: a specific way of moving and a direction.

---

[10] Michael Chekhov, 'Desire for exercising regularly; Characters; Future theatre plans; Fire – Flaming feelings; Archetypal feelings; Right feelings through right means; Eurythmy; Actor-director relationship', 16 January 1938: https://collections.uwindsor.ca/files/original/0b09e77011a6688c0839f8c81be6c62207d6443d.pdf.

The Chekhov work is just as concerned about the inner life of the actor as any acting technique is. It's just that the pathway to this inner life and its doorway are different.

Always allow the movement to inform you. Go into your exploration with the innocence of a child. Ask, sincerely, questions such as, 'What is joy?' Begin to move with a quality of joy and see what comes. See what *meets* you.

Another danger in working with sensation comes from the desire to *show* a certain sensation; the actor's desire to have that sensation register. But of course, there is no way you can reach the depths of a particular feeling or sensation if your only aim is to show it. To work through this, stay with the chosen activity and give yourself over to the activity of doing. Tell yourself, for example, 'I'm going to move my body into the sitting position with a quality of tenderness'. With this work, we are always trying to unite these two entities: our physical and emotional beings.

Exploring through full-bodied movement is the key to investigating qualities and sensations. Explore a range of qualities – playfulness, tenderness, caution – and explore building a series of qualities, continuing to upgrade: quietly-gently-serenely, or slowly-confidently-courageously, or quickly-urgently. Avoid thinking your way into the quality; find it with the body in movement. Movement is always the key with the Chekhov work.

Through the will

In a way, we come at quality and sensation through the will, which has to do with movement, with a gesture, with choice. However, be careful: if you over-exercise the will or really force it, there is no ease, and you will be getting in the way. You don't want ambition on the floor; you don't want to over-exert the will. Instead, you have to allow quality and sensation to unfold.[11]

Chekhov said, 'Everything must be a path to the feelings, if I look upon everything with my whole artistic being'.[12]

---

[11]Quality and Sensation Class with Fern is on page 128. Quality and Sensation through Straight Line and Curved Line with Ted, page 131.
[12]Michael Chekhov, 'Life in our work; Fire – feeling – temperament; Our method awakens feelings; Justify the actor's profession; The actor's sacrifice; Significance

Atmosphere

In our daily life, when we go into certain situations – a hospital, a cathedral, a bookstore or a party – we feel or sense a certain atmosphere. You may have even had the experience of walking into a space, turning around and walking out. Without knowing why, you felt something in that atmosphere that you did not want to participate in.

Fern and Ted advise us that our best training in atmosphere is to listen to atmosphere in our daily lives. We all create atmospheres: in our homes, gardens and cars, and with our friends. Become acutely aware of what is living in the space around you each day. What is the surrounding influence?

Atmosphere is what Chekhov speaks of as the soul of the play.[13] It is an element that brings us right into the present. In working with atmosphere, we are not working with a past experience, something that happened years ago; we have to be living in the present.

Atmosphere is created through the actors collectively putting an imagination into the space. Actors learn to trust that putting their image life into the space can affect the space itself; it can have an effect on the space between each actor. The space between is the substance of the actors' collective imagination. The atmosphere thus created can be subtle, or it can be strong. When you have a group of actors working with, say, moulding, a particular atmosphere is created in the room, because all are engaged in the same activity. The conscious commitment to an activity creates a substance in the space that we call atmosphere.

An actor can create an atmosphere on a stage alone, but a group of actors working, for example, with the intangible of what lives in a cathedral, or a battleground, or in the woods at night can also create an atmosphere that can be deafening. An atmosphere can densify the space. Something moves, something shifts. It's powerful. If as a single actor you bring your character into a company of

---

of costume and make-up', 8 July 1937: https://collections.uwindsor.ca/files/original/98511406491ddf3597c885aabdde8e68952afe33.pdf.
[13]Michael Chekhov, 'Lessons for students in New York class, 7 November 1941: https://collections.uwindsor.ca/chekhov/item/1064.

actors who have created a strong atmosphere, your character will be affected.

The Chekhov work is concerned with intangibles. Atmosphere is ultimately intangible, yet once you begin to experience it, it becomes tangible.

Actors need to be careful in working with atmosphere. What almost always happens initially is that actors turn their experience of atmosphere into behaviour, and begin indicating, demonstrating. In this situation, you must develop a sense of trust, knowing that your image life can affect that which is around you. You can create an image of the woods and live within it. You can create an image of a baby's nursery and live within it. Try taking away the outer image and staying awake to the inner space.

Atmosphere doesn't have to come from a physical place (the woods, a nursery). It could come from the time of day. It can be a colour or a texture: a soft, warm blanket, stinging nettles, a block of ice, a dark heavy cloud or radiant light. It could be laughter, or a musical sound. It can be as beautiful or as ugly, as loud or as soft, as close or as far away as you choose it to be. It could be a feeling, for example, grief. How do you create an atmosphere of grief without feeling that you personally are filled with grief? This is demanding. It requires intense listening, intense inner activity. It is subtle. You need to trust that something will resonate if you're actively engaged in placing an image into the space.

Objective atmospheres

When we speak of an 'objective atmosphere' on stage, we are talking about something that does not belong to us personally. It's something that you walk into; it lives in the space among and between the actors. The objective atmosphere is built together.

Chekhov states that the atmosphere is the best director. He says no director can suggest things which the atmosphere can.[14]

You can develop a deeper understanding of objective atmosphere by coming up against an opposing atmosphere. For example, let's

---

[14]Michael Chekhov, 'Lessons for students in New York class, 7 November 1941: https://collections.uwindsor.ca/chekhov/item/1064.

say you have two different groups of actors: one establishes a New Year's Eve party and the other group has experienced great loss. They come into the space together. What happens if you are an actor within one of these groups? You continue listening to the atmosphere you created, but you are affected by the opposing atmosphere. Two objective atmospheres cannot exist in space simultaneously. One of them will win, not through behaviour but by what is living in the space.

In this situation, if you are intent on holding on to your own atmosphere, you have a problem, because you are not allowing yourself to be affected by the other atmosphere. This becomes a challenge: you need to be open and available to what is literally in the space, rather than feeling compelled to hold on to what you have already established. The task is to be sensitive, to be open to find out what is happening between you and others. You don't know what will happen. Live in the not knowing.

Personal atmosphere

Unlike an objective atmosphere, a personal atmosphere is something you carry around with you. It defines your character. Personal atmosphere exists in the space around the actor. It belongs to you individually. It affects you; it influences you.

Personal atmosphere and objective atmosphere

How does one take a personal atmosphere into an objective atmosphere? Practice. It's essential to develop an experience of each separately. Become adept at creating an objective atmosphere. Work with personal atmosphere until you can feel that you are on solid ground, then seek to bring the two together.

Bringing your character into an atmosphere that is not your own is demanding. When you first approach the task, find something accessible, both as a personal atmosphere and as an objective atmosphere. Play, experiment, explore. Find out for yourself how to juggle these two aspects. Can you bring a personal atmosphere of deep purple into a party atmosphere? Maybe you find it easy. If so, don't deny this. If it's not easy, find images that are accessible to you and find how you can balance one atmosphere with the other.

How does your creative being respond? Seek to be open to having something reveal itself to you, about both personal atmosphere and objective atmosphere.

How to create an atmosphere

As a starting point for atmosphere, ask yourself what the primary qualities of your character are. What is their basic need? How can that need be supported by an atmosphere? Give yourself permission to explore various possibilities. Remember, no work is lost. Discovering who your character is may carry surprises.

Leave yourself open to your creative imagination. Play. The possibilities with both objective and personal atmosphere are limitless.

In creating an atmosphere, it helps to have specific knowledge and experience of atmosphere: for example, the knowledge that we don't move in the same way in a cathedral that we do in a marketplace. A particular smell or a particular sound may help with your imagination. An atmosphere has to be created like a painting or a piece of music.

When you seek to create an atmosphere, you are hoping to be able to receive: to become available to the particular atmosphere that meets you. Seek to be receptive to the images that you put into the space. If you are working with an objective atmosphere, this is a balancing act, because you have to be receptive to your own image and also the image created by the ensemble.

Let's use the example of a personal atmosphere of birdsong. If the space around you is filled with birdsong, how does that affect you? Seek the space to the right and left of you, above and below your physical body, so that you feel you are in a bubble of space. Sense that the space can be filled with an image, an imagination, a specific emotional quality: in this case, birdsong. Play with that sense spatially. Maybe it will be more present in the back-space, or around the head and shoulders, or touching the physical body, or far away.

Play, play, play with your imagination and where it chooses to take you. Be curious in your exploration, instead of feeling the need to find the 'right' atmosphere.[15]

---

[15]Personal Atmosphere with Fern is on page 104. Ensemble and Objective Atmosphere with Ted, page 106.

'Atmosphere gives us the air, the space around us. It coaxes our deeper feelings and emotions, our dreams. . . . Without atmosphere we are imprisoned on the stage.'[16]

Imaginary body

The concept of imaginary body is about discovering and experiencing yourself and your body differently. To find an imaginary body, begin with the image of what your character might look like physically. Then Fern and Ted want us to ask, 'what's the inner, emotional content of that image? What does it feel like?'

Imaginary body can be solely for you, the actor. It can give you a certain quality and substance that feeds the reality of who the character is. In inhabiting an imaginary body, you are experiencing yourself and your own body differently. The images you are engaging with can be potent if you trust the images and trust your imagination.

When you are investigating imaginary body, try not to manipulate your own physical body. If you are working with having no neck, for example, and you try to force your head down into your shoulders, that's not allowing the image to work on you. Imaginary body is subtle, but it can be powerful. You have to bring your whole self – your physical, emotional and spiritual self – to this work.

Imaginary body is another of the intangibles: an image that reflects itself tangibly. When working with an imaginary body, you need to be specific. How long are the arms of your imaginary body? Do the fingers reach beyond the knee? What happens if you have pudgy, huge hands? Or, conversely, tiny, bird-like hands? Commit to staying with the image and exploring the way it reflects itself in your physical body. If you are imagining different hands, do not look at your hands, but live in the imagination of what it is to have these hands that are different from your own. Listen to how that experience affects your inner life. What are the sensations that arise? How do you experience yourself differently?

---

[16]Michael Chekhov, 'Why is a Method Needed in the Theatre of Today?' 7 November 1941: https://collections.uwindsor.ca/files/original/c05e92ea6e8514c94bfdbd2e490 3b58efae0f482.pdf.

Some actors find that they really need to sense their arm before they are able to sense an imaginary arm. You have to be fully present within your own being before you can go to an imaginary body. Then you can surrender your sense of your own arm to your sense of the imaginary arm, and allow that imagination to live in you. Seek to trust and stay with it. The feeling may be subtle. That is to be trusted as well. It does not have to be a significant revelation.

This idea is accessible to different people in different ways. Some people immediately catch on, and others flounder and struggle with how to incorporate it. If you are struggling, Fern and Ted suggest, try to edge your way in. Keep it playful initially, so that you are not turning yourself inside out trying to make believe that your body is one thing or another. At first, just play. What would happen, for example, if your feet were actually two feet long? Don't let yourself get in your own way. Ultimately, you need to be specific and to ground the imaginary body.

We experience imaginary body in our everyday lives, as well. We can be at a party and feel inappropriately dressed. Often, our imaginary body experience in this context is that we feel much smaller than we really are.

In this work, as in other parts of the Chekhov work, what we are seeking is that sweet spot of transformation: to experience ourselves as tall, short, thin, fat or whatever it is we are focusing on.

Imaginary body is closely related to all the work we do on presence, our sense of self. The physical body is very much a part of who we are. It has a lot to do with our confidence, or lack of confidence, in how the rest of the world receives us.

When working with imaginary body, don't judge the body type you're imagining. This gets in the way of discovery, of wrapping yourself up in the image and allowing it to play you. Seek to embrace all aspects of the body, free of judgement.

Playing with imaginary bodies

When you are exploring imaginary bodies, begin with what is possible: perhaps your feet are large, your head is small. You are tall, thin, short or fat. You have no neck or bird-like hands. Then, you'll begin to realize that your only limit is your own imagination. Work with an outrageous feature of the face: a nose three times as large as Cyrano's nose, or a mouth the size of a head. Your skin is green, or your hair is purple. Your neck is a spring, and your head is a bowling ball that keeps falling forward or backward. Your legs are like pipe cleaners. Your arms are strings, and your hands are enormous frying pans hanging from those strings. Your head could be like the end of a Q-tip, and your body enormous. Your feet could be made of very delicate glass, and you have to be careful not to break them.

There is an interplay between text and imaginary body; each influences the other.

You can also put an imaginary body on your acting partner. For example, imagine your acting partner is six feet four and 250 pounds. This will affect your relationship with their character.

Use imaginary body in a moment when your character has just been humiliated, for example. Feel yourself growing smaller physically. The difference between this feeling and a contraction is perhaps subtle, but there is a difference. Alternatively, feel yourself become the dominating force in the room; feel yourself grow physically. You become extremely powerful. Your presence fills the room; your physical body fills the space during the scene or during a speech.

Another way to play with images and our bodies, from a slightly different perspective, is to use the exercise 'Stick, Ball, Veil' (see Part 5).[17] This was one of the first exercises Ted was taught in 1981 by the Dartington ladies at the Chekhov Studio in New York City. Chekhov himself taught this exercise in England.

Moments of change with imaginary body

To use an imaginary body to work with moments of change within a play or for character, you could imagine legs of steel becoming legs of spun glass, resulting in a change from power to powerlessness – a sudden illness or insecurity, or perhaps even a process of ageing. Or you could imagine a short, small, thin body becoming that of a giant – larger than anyone else on the stage.

---

[17]Stick, Ball, Veil Class with Fern, page 140.

When you use this tool, remember that the specificity of your imagination is helpful, and can result in an authentic and powerful moment of change.

The psycho-physical approach, including tools like imaginary bodies, is all about awakening our imaginative consciousness as a creative tool. Any actor with some degree of training or experience in this approach can create an image that will carry power because it is the actor's own image and creation.

Like other Chekhov tools, you should handle imaginary bodies in a way that means you can thoroughly enjoy what you are doing. It's essential to be in love with this work. Of course, as actors, we are serious, and we want that seriousness to always be present in our work, but we should never forget we are players.[18]

'We have the freedom to make the most of the best in all techniques. There are no prohibitions against it. All it takes is a little wisdom, imagination, and courageous experimentation.'[19]

Archetype

An archetype is a typical example of something, or the original model of something from which others are copied. Anyone who is at all familiar with plays or films will be familiar with archetypes like the Queen, the Innocent, the Femme Fatale, the Adolescent, the Charmer, the Bully, the Best Friend. Each of these archetypes has certain identifiable characteristics and qualities.

To work with archetype is to explore character. This exploration may be at the beginning, the middle or the end of a rehearsal period, as you seek to find out who you are inhabiting. It's crucial you allow the archetype to be what it is: to go where it wants to travel, and to reveal what it desires.

Exploring archetypes means exploring the warrior's strength and power, the beggar's survival instinct, the ringleader's ability to keep in charge of proceedings. An archetype can even be an animal: an eagle, a bear, a puppy.

---

[18]Imaginary Body with Fern, page 137.
[19]Charles Leonard, *Michael Chekhov's To the Director and Playwright* (New York: Limelight Editions, 1984).

Working with archetype can also help you with the size of your performance. The archetype adds size and dimension to the character you are playing.

Listening in to the archetype

This is another area in which we engage the art of deep listening. We allow ourselves to be in the presence of the archetype and allow it to reveal itself. Be aware that something is accompanying you: a superhuman presence. Sense that something is walking with you: to the left, to the right and in front of you. Enlarge the essence of your being. The parameter, the periphery, is open to you, and some entity lives within that space. Give yourself over to it; surrender yourself to listening to what's around you. It takes concentration, commitment, interest and curiosity to seek what the archetype has to tell you. Initially, you are met with your own experience and your preconception of who it is. Seek to expand your understanding of that image: the vision of who that being is. Be receptive and explore beyond the known boundaries.

In working with archetypes, we draw upon our creative imagination. As Chekhov says, the image has an independent life to our own as actors.[20] You have to play with the idea of something larger, something more significant, something more powerful than you are in the space around you.

Archetypes might seem simplistic, but they are a gateway to greater complexity. An archetype takes you not into a preconceived idea but to a deeper understanding of who and what you're working with. There is no chart or rule about how you come to it. You just have to be as free as you can with your imagination.

Deciding on an archetype

Don't settle too quickly on a particular archetype. Your first choice may be too literal. As you work with a particular character over time, you will begin to get a better sense of who the character is. Exploring on your feet, working with your instrument, you may find an archetype that speaks to you, that you understand physically and mentally.

---

[20] *To the Actor*, 29.

You may want to explore the opposite of what you think the relevant archetype is, to see if it informs you of some aspect of your character that you haven't probed. It could be that the most obvious archetype is the one that will reveal the least to you about this character. Consider one that is not obvious, or have someone suggest an archetype for you. There may be more than one archetype you want to explore. Allow each to inform the other.

Let's look at the archetype for James Tyrone from *Long Day's Journey into Night*. You can say he's a patriarch. He's an actor, an artist, perhaps dealing with the fact that he grew up poor and became rich.

What about Mary Tyrone from the same play? She's a mother, she's a wife, she's an addict. At this point, you might ask what it is that you, the actor, know the least about; that is where you might want to put your attention. For instance, on Mary's addiction. It might be valuable to work with the gestures of a mother and a wife but dig into what it is to be addicted.

Archetypes and psychological gestures are related. In the archetype, we seek to find the gesture (see the next section in this part, 'Psychological Gesture'). The archetype informs us of its gesture; gesture does not necessarily inform us of archetype. The gesture you're seeking may not fit into the gestures you know. Listen to what gesture suggests itself. Does it have a dominant direction or tempo? A part of the body that it most often engages?

You may be surprised at what the gesture is. We are working out of a part of ourselves that isn't analytical or intellectual. We are working with our bodies and imaginations, and that can reveal untold treasures.

During the rehearsal process, you should work with the archetype enough to have laid a solid foundation, so that the influence of the archetype is available to you during performance. You may find that you do not call upon it during the performance, but you may also find that there is a specific moment when it becomes essential to you; it fulfils a need. Openness to this requires you to be present at every moment. Training in the Chekhov work is always about seeking to be present to what *is*, in the moment.

The archetype can also help you find the imaginary centre and the imaginary body of your character, and inform you of your character's relationship to other characters, both in the rehearsal room and during performance.[21]

---

[21] Archetype Class with Fern, page 142.

Following is a list of archetypes, which is by no means exhaustive. Joanna Merlin and Dawn Arnold, director of Moving Dock Theatre in Chicago, contributed to this list. Note that the list has historical origins; some of these terms may seem to you not to be in line with the terminology or sense of morality of today.

Remember that these archetypes are not multi-dimensional characters. They are starting points, to activate us as actors and assist in the art of transformation. Let this list whet your appetite: treat it as something to play with as you explore character.

ADDICT
ADOLESCENT
ADVOCATE
ALCHEMIST
AMBASSADOR
ANGEL
ATHLETE
AVENGER
BABY
BACKSTABBER
BASTARD
BAT BOY
BEGGAR
BELIEVER
BEST FRIEND
BLACK WIDOW
BOSS
BULLY
CAREGIVER
CARETAKER
CAT
CHARMER
CHIEF

CHILD / WOUNDED CHILD
CLOWN
COMPANION
COWARD
CREATOR
CRIPPLE
CRUSADER
DAMSEL
DANDY
DESTROYER
DETECTIVE
DEVIL
DILETTANTE
DISCIPLE
DOG
DON JUAN
EMPRESS
ENSLAVED PERSON
EVANGELIST
EVIL GENIUS
EXORCIST

FANATIC
FATHER
FEMME FATALE
FIRECRACKER
FOOL
FREE SPIRIT
FRIEND
GAMBLER
GENERAL
GENIUS
GOSSIP
GUIDE
HEALER
HEDONIST
HERMIT
HERO
INNOCENT
INVADER
INVENTOR
JUDGE
KING
KNIGHT
LAWYER

LEADER	POSSESSED	SHARK
LIBERATOR	PRIEST	SNAKE
LIBRARIAN	PRINCE	SOLDIER
LOST SOUL	PRINCESS	SPUNKY KID
LOVER	PRISONER	STAR
LUNATIC	PROFESSOR	STORYTELLER
MAGICIAN	PROM QUEEN	STUDENT
MARTYR	PROSTITUTE	SWASHBUCKLER
MATRIARCH	QUEEN	TEACHER
MENTOR	REBEL	TERRORIST
MESSIAH	RESCUER	THIEF
MISER	RINGMASTER	TRAITOR
MONK	RULER	TRICKSTER
MOTHER	SABOTEUR	TYRANT
MYSTIC	SADIST	VAMPIRE
NETWORKER	SAINT	VICTIM
NURTURER	SAMARITAN	VIRGIN
ORPHAN	SCEPTIC	VIRTUOUS WOMAN
OUTCAST	SCHOLAR	VISIONARY
OUTSIDER	SCRIBE	WAIF
PARASITE	SEDUCTRESS	WARRIOR
PATIENT	SEEKER	WOUNDED HEALER
PIONEER	SERVANT	
POET	SERVANT OF GOD	
POLITICIAN	SHAPESHIFTER	

'There is nothing more pleasant than to get a little contact with the archetype – it is a blessing – it is artistic bliss.'[22]

---

[22] Michael Chekhov, 'The archetype', 17 February 1941: https://collections.uwindsor.ca/files/original/5a1a27b91b4c1b6286014c7db247496f62ccbaf1.pdf.

Psychological gesture

Finally, the jewel in the crown of the Chekhov canon: psychological gesture. Psychological gesture is *gesture done in an archetypal way, influenced by a specific quality.*

Before we delve into the foundations of psychological gesture and discuss how we use and apply this idea, we need to look at what gesture is.

The difference between movement and gesture

Primarily, the difference between movement and gesture is intention. What is it you want? What is it you want to do? What is it you want, need, desire to do to the other person? It is in asking and answering these questions that gesture comes about.

An impulse – to reject, to comfort, to seize, to hit, to caress, to embrace – is translated into action, and that action requires physical movement, which is a gesture. When we speak about gesture, we often use the word 'impulse', and most impulses come out of information. We are talking about the invisible becoming visible, the intangible becoming tangible. That which we have in our desire body gives rise to impulse. It is invisible before it becomes a physical gesture.

Once you begin to realize what gesture is, you become aware that gesture is around you everywhere, in all parts of your life. We are always in gesture. What we are trying to do is to make all that gesture conscious and available. In the Chekhov work, we go back to this idea that we are gestural beings again and again.

How to develop a psychological gesture

Chekhov tells us in *To the Actor* that psychological gesture is archetypal.[23] In making an archetypal gesture, you are using as much space and as much of your body as you can, without letting unnecessary tension in. Fern and Ted tell us, the heels of your

---

[23]*To the Actor*, 70.

feet, somehow, are involved in executing the gesture. 'It's a great big granddaddy gesture that you ultimately take inward, where it becomes the execution of your objective.'

To avoid playing the idea of a gesture, you do it outwardly repeatedly, so it stirs the will and that awakens something within. It is this inner activity that makes the invisible visible. Eventually, you conceal the outward gesture; it becomes your actor's secret. Its living presence remains within you as an emotional state. This is a big step. There is still movement, but it's now inner movement. It still affects you physically and emotionally.

A true psychological gesture is *an inner gesture*.

A gesture can have movement, direction and intention, without being psychological. To be a psychological gesture, it has to have a *quality*. We talk about the gesture being the *what*, the intention being the *why* and the quality being the *how*. The quality can be, for example, sorrow, joy or caution. The quality completes the intention. When we add quality, the how (for example, *'sadly'*) and the what (for example, *'pull'*) become one unit.

If quality is one of the foundations of the psychological gesture, another is *tempo*. What tempo is the gesture in? For example, an inner gesture of 'pull' can be slow and deliberate, and very threatening. If you increase that tempo, the pull becomes frantic.

Another one of the foundations of psychological gesture is *radiation*: with intention, the gesture radiates beyond the bounds of the human body. Remember, intention is what makes gesture different from movement.

A final foundation is *direction*. Is the gesture a pull going into the front-space, or the back-space? Does it go up, or down?

To the Actor mentions gestures in broad terms: push, pull, lift, smash, penetrate and throw. Ted and Fern start with these and add reach, open, close, punch and tear. A psychological gesture however is not limited to what is described as archetypal gestures in Michael Chekhov's book (push, pull, wring, etc.). It is in fact not limited to any verb or action word. It can be much more poetic. The example Chekhov gives us is reaching out and returning empty-handed. Or his example of a character forcibly clawing down inspiration from the heavens.

You may want to start with reach, as it is accessible, and it comes right out of the middle. As you move into the world of gesture, you can explore into slap, kick, strike, caress, crush. There is no limit to the number and type of gestures you can play with.

The following is a list of gestures accompanied by a list of qualities/sensations that Fern and Ted use to help tweak your imagination.

Gestures	Qualities/Sensations
PUSH	SADNESS
PULL	CAUTION
OPEN	FEAR
CLOSE	JOY
PENETRATE	ANGER
THROW	DESPERATION
SMASH	WARMTH
LIFT	DECISIVE
TEAR	GENTLE
PUNCH	CAREFULNESS
EMBRACE	COURAGEOUS
WRING	TENDERLY
	QUIETLY
	VIOLENTLY
	TIMIDLY
	POWERFULLY
	FORCEFULLY
	CONFIDENTLY
	SERENELY
	GENEROUSLY
	COLOURS

It isn't helpful to overly theorize the concept of gestures: it can't be nailed to the ground, because a push from one actor is different to a push from another actor. It is also important to remember that Michael Chekhov described the psychological gesture as the intuitive invention of the individual actor: Who can tell whether the gesture is the right one? No-one but the actor.

Your psychological gesture must be strong, simple and well-formed. Ask questions like 'What do I want?' 'What do I want to do to this person?' Or 'What do I want to make this person do?'

To truly make a psychological gesture takes the fullness of the body. You are at one with every aspect of your body, you are at one with the space, and you join the body with the space, so that all of you is engaged.

In working with gestures, you are looking to create one that has a beginning, middle and end. The beginning is the impulse. The gesture itself is the middle. The end is what happens after, which we ride on, sustaining the gesture. This isn't an unnatural thing: any big gesture that we make in life remains for a while after it is made. You don't want to get to the end of the gesture too quickly; enjoy the journey, participating inwardly in the movement of the gesture. If you are seeking for the gesture to have its full effect only when you reach the end, you might have robbed yourself of the experience of the gesture.

How to use psychological gesture

A psychological gesture can define a character. It can be your through-line throughout the play. It can be relational in the moment. It can activate a moment between you and your acting partner.

You are *not* defined or limited to *one* gesture throughout a play. If you do decide to stick with one gesture, maybe the quality, or the basic intention, changes. For example:

- the quality of a *pulling* gesture changes from *gently* (to comfort) to *powerfully* (to seduce)
- the quality of an *embrace* gesture changes from *gently* (to protect) to *aggressively* (to possess)
- the quality of a *reaching* gesture changes from *longingly* (to plead/seek help) to *angrily* (to seize power)
- the quality of a *pushing* gesture changes from *angrily* (to harm) to *cautiously* (to distance oneself)
- the quality of a *penetrating* gesture changes from *sadly* (to reach, understand) to *determinedly* (to convince or dominate)

Like all the elements of the Chekhov work, gesture isn't some mechanical thing that we do. Rather, the life within us gives life to the character. You have to be inwardly active, and there is no better way to be inwardly active than with an inner gesture.

Psychological gesture is the most misunderstood aspect of the Chekhov work. It seems esoteric, but Fern and Ted tell us it's really very simple. Theatre is gestural. A gesture towards or away from your acting partner has everything to do with your intention. Fern and Ted have expressed the wish that more actors had a chance to really experience how available psychological gesture is. We live in gesture every day: as we walk down the street; as we deal with people we love or people we don't like. What Chekhov has done is develop a method where that becomes conscious.

With the Chekhov work, gesture is the key to the kingdom. It's where the life is. To make a gesture is to fulfil an intention, a need, a desire.[24]

Psychological gesture can give you a ground on which to stand. When you have found the gesture, you're living in something that is a language of its own. That's where the life is. It's a huge gift. The question is always 'What is the life I'm looking for in portraying this character?'

---

[24] Awakening to Gesture Class with Fern, page 144. The Psychological Gesture: Adding Quality and Gesture with Fern, page 147. Using Mask to Explore Archetypal Gesture with Ted, page 148.

Part 4

Putting the tools to use

After studying with Ted and Fern in America, I returned to Australia. I felt that I now had many choices at my fingertips: an embarrassment of riches, if you will. A few months later, though, I found myself in a rehearsal room with one burning question: how was I to integrate these tools into my practice and apply them in the fast-paced world of putting on a show? Where was my starting point? How did I know what to include and what to leave out when I was creating a character and telling a story? How many tools were too little, and how many too many? Classes were one thing; it was suddenly clear to me that rehearsals were another beast entirely.

This part of the book aims to answer the questions I've posed just above, by taking you into the rehearsal room – and onto the stage – with Fern and Ted themselves. In a practical sense, it gives you guidance, in Fern and Ted's own words, on how to put these powerful tools in to practice.

It's important to highlight that there is no need to separate a rehearsal tool from what we bring on to the stage, whether for a few performances or for a long run. Whatever you choose to do in rehearsal is to enliven you, to awaken you to activity, which enables you to bring life onto the stage.

Ted says:

> I don't have a system that always works for me during rehearsals. My process varies with each role and play. I simply need to read the words out loud. I may come into the first rehearsal with an idea or two, but I am always looking at rehearsals as the place to

find out, whether I'm rehearsing with The Actors' Ensemble or with another company not fluent in the Chekhov practice.

A thorough physical warm-up is essential for me, to rid myself of those places of resistance and where my physical and inner life are not two separate entities. Then I feel able to be creative and can do the Chekhov work more fully. At the beginning of any rehearsal period, it's always of great benefit to me to be aware of the condition of my instrument. To do whatever I need to bring consciousness to the physical form. From this embodiment can come the freedom I need to be genuinely creative.

There are times when I just have to start moving. Then, suddenly, I may find that I'm much more available to what's happening inwardly, emotionally.

The one aspect of the work I use more than any other is the centre of the characters' being: their centre of energy. That alive place out of which the character speaks and moves. I always find that the centre gets me into a place, at least in the beginning of rehearsals, between myself and the character. Then it can be the bridge for that character becoming me. That's not true for every actor, but that's true for me. It's a visceral, doable, immediate part of the work that can take me somewhere.

Some roles are much more of a reach for me, in which case I need to find the character physically – perhaps through image, imaginary body, the walk, the stance, mannerisms, any of the transformative elements of the work that Chekhov has given us.

If it is a role I relate immediately to, I may want to work off of my acting partners, in which case, radiating and receiving connects me, right from the beginning, to that relationship. Or I might consider what my character's gesture is toward my acting partner. From there, I begin to develop it through quality and tempo.

Then there are other elements I love working from as an opening: circumstances, for instance, or specific moments which attract me, where I might engage in a slow or strong change of centre. Or engage in an inner play of expanding and contracting.

Fern says:

I start rehearsals with what is with me, with my body, going from movement to stillness so I can really stop and quietly tune in to what is going on. I inch my way in, taking all the time necessary to find how present I can be to myself, my environment, the others who may be in the space with me, and the fullness of my body.

I also bring to consciousness the three physical centres of vitality, clarity and openness, to find some sense of impulse within me. There is no one way in. I may begin with ease and movement, incorporating more and more of the physical body. I may start with softening the body and sensing its weight. To state a process that goes step by step is misleading. What is essential is to start with where I am and be led by needs, wants and desires that may arise.

Gradually, I move into being receptive to the character, listening to what is in the space around me so the character can begin to inform me. Chekhov tells us the character makes the choice, not the actor. I seek to allow the character to play around me and suggest a quality of movement, a gesture, an imaginary centre. An imagination and images may present themselves, and the decision must be made at some point as to what needs to be taken seriously and followed. I am constantly seeking a meeting with the character to discover who that person is. Somehow the actor and the character meet one another. Something then lives in the atmosphere that invites specific actions, relationships and directions.

Because I have trained in this work for years, suggestions and choices begin to present themselves. In no way am I implying that there wasn't an awful lot of conscious work to be done; it's just that the revelation of who these women were wasn't kept as a secret from me.

The last several characters I have played spoke loudly and clearly as they began to reveal themselves. I'm learning and trusting to get out of the way. The older I get, the less I nail anything down. I acknowledge that there is a certain mystery to the creative process.

I remind myself that it's okay to flounder, to not know, and to be willing to stay with the not knowing. That can be very painful and frustrating at times. I've found that if I force a choice out of fear that nothing is happening, it won't get me anywhere. This doesn't negate trying out different choices. There is a difference between experimenting, exploring and investigating a choice and demanding it be the right one. I can try something and see how far it takes me – if it informs me of something.

It's mainly living with your instrument and seeing what it has to say to you about a particular situation. Allowing the images, the imagination within that, to live and inform you of the direction. Here, presence comes into play. What is it to be present, fully conscious in every part of your being, to both yourself and your surroundings? Perhaps that's the starting point for any rehearsal and any classwork – for everything really – being present.

The first read of a play

When we first read a play, we should not necessarily be looking for anything except the story itself. Out of this story, images will arise.

As you read, you absorb the basic information about the story: how it is being told and by whom. You give attention to sensations and images. Questions may arise. You live through the play in your imagination, in some way.

When you finish reading the play, be aware that you have just gone through something. You have lived through that situation; you have lived through those characters, relationships and conflicts. Listen to what that experience stirred in you, and don't ask too much of yourself. How did that experience engage your imagination, your sense of life? Seek to enjoy what the playwright has to say, free of judgement or demand.

Working with images

Fern says:

Images have given me life for characters that would otherwise have been inaccessible. In *Dandelion Wine* by Ray Bradbury, I had a very long list of things and events, and I gave each of them a specific image, which intercepted the fear of not being able to remember each item, and instead replaced it with pleasure.

At a certain point in *Mrs Ripley's Trip*, I had to move through a powerful snowstorm. How much of that is image, imagination, gesture and quality of movement? The gesture arrives out of the storm I'm in. The storm comes out of my imagination. The image itself brings an atmosphere.

In *The Trip to Bountiful*, Carrie Watts, the character I played, spends a considerable amount of time recalling long-ago memories. I formed an image for each memory. Images provide an avenue to enter which is filled with riches. An image has an independent life and can lead you. It can guide you and bring you to unknown places.

You may go through your script looking for images. Maybe the written word calls up an image within you.

In the Ripley stories (*Mrs Ripley's Trip* and *Uncle Ethan Ripley*), we had two chairs on an otherwise empty stage. Our image life created an indoor space with a kitchen, table, wood-burning cook stove, a working cabinet. There was an outdoor space, cold winter weather, a cornfield, horses, a road leading to town and a snowstorm.

During rehearsals with The Actors' Ensemble, we worked a great deal with the contrasting atmospheres of indoors and outdoors; with the far-off horizon. We had an image of a vast Iowa prairie and the image of outside/inside. There was often the sensation of expanding and contracting and warmth or cold, warmth being in the contracting and cold being in the expansion. We would work in rehearsals with The Ensemble for long periods, coming out of a little cabin, into the wagon, out of the farm, as we drove to town with the sky above us.

Ted says:

I did a piece from *The Grand Inquisitor*, out of *The Brothers Karamazov*, and I struggled. One thing I did was to find the character's face. I remember working by myself in a dark basement room; no lights were on, and I worked. I didn't sit down and work with an image and incorporate the image; I worked on my feet with the image in that room. It was very particular, and it was a specific image I was working with.

Fern and I have both done theatre pieces where there has been a lot of narration. It's essential to have images of what you are seeing or what you are asking the audience to see. The more specific the images can be, the more powerful they are.

We used to often close our eyes, if we were working on a character, and see if we could see how the character would walk or dress. Or if we could even hear the character's voice. You may get not a full image, but a sense of something; maybe just a colour. Or a piece of fabric that this person was wearing. We both learned to trust that whatever image comes is worth investigating, instead of throwing it aside and saying, 'Oh no, what has that got to do with this character?' It will have something to do with the character; otherwise it wouldn't have come up.

Layering the tools

An actor makes a choice of a tool or tools in seeking transformation. This defines the character, and, of necessity, it defines how the character will respond to other characters.

Fern says:

You don't want anything that divides you from your acting partner in rehearsal or in performance. How can you work with a choice you've made and not lose contact with your acting partner? You hold the choice as you would hold a thought while speaking to a friend. You communicate to your acting partner through the choice. No choice needs ever separate you from your acting partners, unless that separation is a choice. The actor remains open to listening and receiving at all times.

It's important to focus on one choice at a time with this work. Otherwise it can become overwhelming.

Layering means that I will investigate an aspect of the work, and then I will let it go. I'll see where it takes me, whether it feeds me or not, and then I will let it go and try another aspect. Then I can either marry them or not.

It's impossible to have an imaginary centre, an imaginary body, a quality of movement and a gesture. Dig deep and find out the primary quality. Maybe the imaginary body attracts the centre: stay with the imaginary body. The centre is there, but the focus is on the imaginary body.

Each choice can be touched on lightly or thoroughly penetrated. You may find that other aspects of the work come to meet the particular tool you are choosing to engage with. However, it is important to be willing to stay with one primary focus of attention and not be drawn into many different directions where there is no focus. It could be that the imaginary body, for example, is all you need to fulfil the transformation you are seeking.

Ted says:

An ideal rehearsal session is where you are allowed by the director to investigate, to try. For the day, just work with one particular thing. You don't have to share with the director what it is or what you are doing. Just play. Experiment.

Once I have explored each element individually, I might choose to combine them. It is so satisfying when you bring in the centre with the imaginary body. See how they converse with each other. Then you might realise that it's not really the centre you should be working with. All of this investigative work is not a matter of, 'I did this, and I failed.' You are investigating; you are integrating. You are always there at the centre of it, going, 'yes, these things work together,' or, 'no, they don't.' What you are doing is finding out something about this character that you didn't know before.

The aim is, by marrying these elements, to allow them to become one thing. Your body knows how to make that adjustment. In the Chekhov work, we reconstruct ourselves. If you are working with an imaginary body, an imaginary centre and a quality of movement, as an example, those things want to harmonise. The self and the body are not two separate entities. You need to blend those colours into each other to integrate them. You want to be one person.

For any one part, you can use as many tools as you can manage. Fern and Ted suggest that a young actor shouldn't arrive at too many choices. You don't want to burden yourself with so many choices that you are paralyzed by them.

When you are initially encountering a character, you play with many different elements of the work. You ask questions like, for example, 'does a certain quality of movement give me anything or take me anywhere?'

Eventually, one tool, maybe two, is really going to speak to you. That element takes over and says, 'you need to deepen this to see where it can take you'. You are on your feet, investigating, exploring. You might think that you will start working with one, and it becomes another; a centre becomes an archetype, for example. Allow your instrument to guide you.

Fern says:

I was working on the play *For the Pleasure of Seeing Her Again* and I approached everything through image. I physicalised the image in the space. I would take an image and act it out repeatedly, bringing the images to life, so they didn't remain an idea. It was only one aspect of the work, yet, it was everything.

In playing the chorus in *Antigone*, I primarily stayed with the archetype of the ringleader. It gave me the gesture to dominate the space and surround and gather the other actors on stage. Sometimes I would penetrate, sometimes reach and touch, but it always came out of the archetype of the ringleader. I also connected strongly to the centre in the chest.

In *Mrs Ripley's Trip*, a story we have dramatized and put on the stage for over 30 years, the choices keep evolving, and more and more layers are added. Over the years, I have worked with several things. The primary one, in the beginning, was gesture. It was a push, regardless of what obstacle came for the character. It was powerful, and that carried me throughout the whole play. I also worked with contraction, and my partner was expanded, so that I had an image at times of being a dried-up prune to a much larger acting partner. Because of the fatigue of the character, I also worked with weight. Different things became dominant in each performance over the years. The centre was in the belly, because of the character's will. I worked with stiffness of the joints in the ankles and the knees. I worked with flat feet. The imaginary body was short and contracted.

I'm not saying that I worked on all of these things all of the time. Over the years, different elements have come. At one point, I might totally focus on the gesture, and at another time the centre in the belly.

Once, I played a mermaid, in one of Thornton Wilder's three-minute plays, and the character was soulless. It was an interesting challenge. It hit me during rehearsals that the character neither radiates nor receives, and I found a place within that felt soulless. This was particular to my experience. It worked for me but might not necessarily work for another actor.

Ted says:

When creating Creon in Anouilh's *Antigone*, I worked with several choices. Even in performance, I was trying different choices on different nights. I would try finding centres of authority; having a high centre, somewhere between the chin and the collarbone, gave the character a sense of haughtiness.

There were moments when Creon tries to be reasonable and tries to reach Antigone, and my centre was in the centre of the chest and was a centre of light. I used lots of different gestures: penetrating, dominating, trying to open. In the last performance, I found something that just came to me right before my first entrance, the hands in relation to the space. What it gave me was, 'I'm in charge here. I own this space. I am the king of Thebes.' I felt there was a fundamental change for that performance.

After the news came that Haemon, my son, had killed himself, I worked with a sense of emptiness. I wasn't going for sorrow, although there were times when tears came. I had to constantly work to find what it is to be empty. I was, however, very much in the present. There were times in the play when I had to put that imaginary crown on my head as an image – working for authority and presence. I came at it from many different angles, sometimes with centre and quality, sometimes with psychological gestures and many, many images.

With my role in *Mrs Ripley's Trip*, I was working with my centre being in the earth, like I was ploughing when I moved. Then I primarily worked with the gesture, and then worked my way through something dense. The last couple of times I have performed it, I have worked very much with my own body: the aching in my joints. The overall impression of how stiff my fingers are. The knees, the hips, the fingers and the hands. It gave me a real sense of age.

We did some work with costumes in *Washington Square*. We realised that once we were on our feet with the piece, we would have to work with imaginary nineteenth-century costumes. It was revelatory. I considered what was around the wrists. How high was the collar? I tried to work with it like an imaginary body.[1]

Working with limited time

If you are working with limited time (for example, you need to present something quickly), Ted and Fern suggest choosing only one element of the work. Avoid asking too much of yourself as an actor and aim to truly penetrate, to the best of your ability, the choice that interests you, that you are curious about or that is doable for you. Do one thing as fully as you can. Practise. Eliminate the need to make it right. Seek the life you can discover in your one choice and find out where it leads you.

Qualities and sensations, and staccato and legato, are tools that you might find more immediate. Be careful, though. It is easy to apply quality and sensation superficially. Work on really engaging in seeking the sensation through doing.

---

[1] Choices, Contact and Point of Focus Class with Ted is on page 149.

Your one element might be the character's centre. This can be efficient because it may lead to intention and gesture.

An actor experienced in the Chekhov work might use more than one tool in this situation, and be able to effectively apply them very quickly: for example, a combination of imaginary body and imaginary centre, imaginary centre and quality of movement, or quality of movement and psychological gesture.

To someone who has had very little training in the Chekhov work, Fern and Ted share the most available tools are imaginary centre, quality of movement, radiating and receiving, and expanding and contracting. Ultimately, one would do well to stay with radiating and receiving. True acting is always a constant exchange of those two.

Remember, the work doesn't stop with opening night. Chekhov himself found many things in performance that ended up being the choices that really shaped the role.

Camera work

The difference between live theatre and film often has to do with the size and execution of an actor's choices; this is true of any acting method, not just the Chekhov work. Following any process to its ultimate destination and goal is powerful on stage and is doubly so on film. In both a live theatre and film context, your choices and their execution must be authentic; the element of truth must be present in both.

In film acting, there is an excellent opportunity to really take a gesture or a change of centre deeply inside yourself and to trust it. Following the process of the inner movement of a psychological gesture or a changing centre can be powerful on screen. It's visceral.

The one advantage of acting for film is spontaneity; it's fresh, last-minute, immediate. The actor doesn't have too much time to get into their heads with film acting. As the actor, in working with that spontaneity, you could be asking yourself what inner gesture you are making towards your acting partner. Do you want to embrace them? Do you want to slowly push them away?

Images are also helpful here. Many film actors have wonderful access to their image life. You might work on an imagined inner activity, like something dangerous in your back-space that's getting closer. Or is all of your energy pouring down into your stomach – or out the top of your head? You may imagine that the upper part of your body is becoming less and less alive.

Another imagined inner activity could be that you are plunging a knife right into their heart when you are speaking to them. Or you could feel that the space you are in is surrounded by a certain sound, or a certain colour, which would give it a certain atmosphere that is living between you.

Moments of change

Some tools are particularly valuable for working with moments of change for a character during a play.

Fern and Ted tell us, one is a change of centre. It could simply be a change of location: a high centre to a low centre, for example. A centre in the head might sink to the stomach or a centre in the chest might rise above the head.

Such changes will naturally effect a different change in each person, depending on the character, the circumstances of the play and the actor.

You could also work with a change in tempo, or a change in the quality of a gesture, as we've talked about above.

Any change in your imaginary body would change your sense of self. Remember that these examples require specificity in their application, resulting in artistic authenticity and truth.

Changes can also result from working with a *quick change* of tempo, a *slow shift* in a personal atmosphere or a straight/curved line.

Bringing the technique onto the stage

Ted says:

We don't bring a technique on to the stage; we bring our human processes on to the stage.

These exercises that we practise were developed by Michael Chekhov to open the door, in a conscious way, to what remains mainly unconscious in our daily lives. Expanding and contracting; living a gestural life that consists of reaching, pushing away, pulling towards, embracing, penetrating, and so on was our first language, before we had the words for our wishes and concerns.

Through Chekhov's exercises, we learn to recognise those moments of unconscious inner activity which carry such power of expression in our daily life – why would we not bring this life on to the stage?

Chekhov's psycho-physical exercises become a means of expressing the moment: when the character you're playing reveals to the audience a particular human experience. You can bring your humanity to that moment – a process – to locate, execute and express what that moment is asking of you, of the character.

You don't locate a technique; you locate what is in you, which a technique has revealed as a daily human process. What we hope to bring on to the stage is our humanity.

Actors often find that they discover something in front of an audience that they never discovered in rehearsals. When you are on stage, the audience is speaking to you. The audience begins to tell you who you are as a character and tells you the relationship between you and others. The performance is never complete until it's before an audience. The audience is the co-creator.

Part 5

Class exercises

This section presents transcripts of Fern and Ted's classes, under headings that reflect the essential and transformative tools presented in earlier parts, in similar order.

It is important to note that Fern and Ted consistently use three of the classes that appear here as 'warm-up' classes:

'Radiating and Receiving'
'Touch and Contact'
'The Three Centres'.[1]

These classes act as an entry point to the Chekhov work; they help students wake up and warm up their bodies and act as a gateway to the technique (as well as being tools in and of themselves). You may wish to start with one of these classes.

Actors – or teachers of actors – can use these classes as a guide or springboard. They will be most useful to a group, as many involve working with partners. If you are working in a group, you may wish to designate one of your number to simply read the instructions that appear here – or use them as a jumping-off point. Use the line breaks as pauses to allow others to receive an idea or to engage in a particular activity.

---

[1]Radiating and Receiving Class with Fern is on page 83, Touch and Contact Class with Ted, page 85 and The Three Centres Class with Ted is on page 86.

When Ted and Fern are teaching, their general practice is to guide their students through the exercises and then, towards the conclusion of the class, to describe the tool that has been practised and field questions. The transcripts here have been edited to the extent that a description of a tool often appears within the exercise, to serve as a reminder of the fuller descriptions given above in this book. This will mean that, in a class situation, the student actor will have a more embodied and comprehensive experience.

The essentials

Expanding and contracting – a beginner's class

Start from a contracted position by bringing the arms closely into the torso. Press them into the upper part of the body while bending slightly forward at the same time.

From here, you will move outward into an expansion.

Slowly straighten your curved spine as you extend the arms out and up, while moving the legs out to the side into a full-body expansion.

Then bring the arms and legs back into the contracted position.

Then, again, out into the expanded position.

This simple physical movement will awaken a familiar human experience of inner emotional expansion, such as elation, fear, anger or surprise. Allow the experience to lead you where it will, where it wants to. Keep the tempo to one that will enable and allow inner participation.

Take your time.

Give yourself the time to find the emotional content of contracting, beginning with its opposite; from an expanding position, come to a contracting position.

Place the arms and legs comfortably out to the side. Begin slowly to draw them into the body, while slowly bending slightly forward.

After several attempts, allow yourself to sink down to one knee – then up very quickly to the expanding position, noticing the sudden change of your inward response.

Take the time to explore this new dynamic of both contracting and expanding; the body moves down to the floor and then quickly into a more powerful expansion.

Let's add another condition to these two primary elements of expanding and contracting: space and periphery.

Surround yourself with a given periphery. It could be the perimeter of the room or even beyond the room.

Expand slowly out to that imaginary periphery, right out into space. A broad and wide inner expansion will result. Then drop the arms while existing in that new sense of presence.

Now, move about the room. Carry with you the sense that you fill the room, fill the space.

Walk out of the room and re-enter it with this new sense of heightened presence. Open the centre of the chest as you carry yourself about the space.

Now, just walk out of that expansion, let it go. Let's look at some other possibilities of what an expansion could be.

Find your periphery again. From a neutral position, prepare to expand. I will clap as a signal to move quickly out in space in a staccato expansion. (Clap)

Now, this time let the quick staccato movement give rise to anger while shouting the words, 'Stop it!' (Clap)

Stay in the fire of the anger while moving forward several steps – let the quality of the movement itself take you to that emotional state. Don't act anger; don't push it.

Just walk out of it now, take several breaths, shake the hands and the arms, let it go.

Now let's engage in a slow, meditative expansion. Don't forget your periphery; where is it?

Begin on your own to allow the movement of the expansion to become a growing *fear*, slowly.

Stay in that expansive state, moving about the room, carrying the growing fear that the movement has given rise to.

Stop occasionally and look behind you. Move slowly forward.

Sit slowly in a chair. Rise slowly to a standing position. This is all done with a continuing inner movement of expanding.

Bring the body into movement from an upright position into a slow expansion out to the given periphery.

When this is achieved, begin slowly to draw away from that periphery, bringing the arms into the torso, sinking down to one knee, and growing smaller inwardly. As you reach that final physical position, you are continuing the inner movement and sensation of contracting while you're engaged in finding that inner response and movement.

Rise and walk about the room.

If you are looking down at the floor, at some point, try raising your gaze to look out into the forward space while drawing into yourself.

What is the effect of that change?

Ask someone near you for directions. How does the presence of another person affect your inner state?

Try different activities with different physical tempos. Allow the inward contracting action to inform you. The movement is your teacher.

Experiment with text.

Give yourself permission to return to the outward movement of contracting or expanding. The movement always continues. It always remains active.

Take some time on your own to explore these two elements, expanding and contracting. Investigate. Explore.

Expanding and contracting – advanced

Start from a contracted position by bringing the arms closely into the torso, pressing into the upper part of the body, bending slightly forward.

Now, straighten your curved spine as you extend the arms out and upward, while also moving the legs out to the side into a full-body expansion.

Bring the arms and legs back into the contracted position. Then out again into a position of expansion.

Stay for a time in each position before completing its opposite.

The completed position will bring a bodily and inner sensation of being contracted or expanded.

Allow yourself to abide for a time in each state of being: contracted or expanded. Going from one to the other. Testing it through working with text.

Now let's go back to the form of the activity itself, starting in a contracted position and moving outward into the movement of expansion. Allow the movement itself to be your focus – not the final position, but the activity of expanding.

When you've reached the peak of the expanded movement, drop the outward physical movement of the arms and legs while retaining the inward movement – walk about the space, inwardly expanding.

Now, reverse it. Bring the arms towards the body slowly into a continuing contrasting movement: that of contracting. Again, allow the movement itself to be your primary focus – so that it becomes a self-willed activity of contracting into yourself.

I'm going to give you a situation, in which these extremes can be applied.

You enter the stage in a state of expanding. You notice an unopened letter. You open it and read. As you read its contents, you begin the inner activity of contracting. When the letter has been read, you drop it to the floor and slowly exit while contracting.

Contracting is a continuing process. As you exit, you are actively engaged in that continuing process of contracting.

Let go of the work, clear yourself and give some thought to your exploration.

Staying with this scenario, this time you enter with an inner activity of contracting which evolves into expanding as you take in the letter's content. You leave the stage quickly with the letter.

Opening and closing gestures, or expanding and contracting?

There is a tendency to equate expanding and contracting with opening and closing.

We suggest that expanding and contracting relates to the degree of outer space one chooses to occupy; opening and closing are related to inner space.

Let's see if you can give yourself the freedom and opportunity to explore this possibility.

Find a partner. Begin throwing a ball to each other. Live into and sense the exchange that is taking place between you. A giving, a receiving. What needs to happen inwardly to enable you to catch the ball and truly receive it?

Stay with this as a want, a wish – to receive.

Find the outer gesture that will create a space within you that will allow you to generously take in what is given.

Open the arms wide and listen to the inner feeling response to that gesture.

Repeat it several times and see if something begins to stir, perhaps in the area of the ideal centre.

Can you allow yourself to sense – feel into – what it is to open inwardly and be available?

When the ball is sent to you, widen the arms and shoulders, first outwardly and then with the invisible arms and shoulders, allowing the ideal centre to be available to receive.

You are seeking to find a space within that is open.

Resist feeling you have to talk yourself into being open.

Be generous; give yourself the opportunity of staying in the process of seeking just that.

Let go of your partner and the ball and move through the space, moving in and out of outwardly expressing the gesture of being open and engaging in the inner activity accompanying that.

What is it to carry being open inwardly?

Now we are going to explore the opposite gesture. Bring the arms close to your sides and the legs close together, and lower the head. Allow the body to be loose and make the gesture of closing with ease. Let the inner response evolve as you execute this outer gesture repeatedly.

As you repeat the gesture, listen to what the inner feeling experience/sensation is, free of demand, to discover and experience what it is to close inwardly.

Seek the difference, although it may be subtle, between expanding and contracting, which has to do with outer space, and opening and closing, which has to do with inner space.

This is a process worthy of exploration. See what you can discover for yourself. Can you experience these as related but different activities?

Of course, it is possible to unite both the inner and outer space to open and expand, close and contract. However, the two are not always synonymous. You can expand and be closed; you can contract and be open. It is possible to explode in anger, expanding, and be closed within. It is possible to contract within but to be open to the beauty of the sunset.

Qualities of movement – a beginner's class

Moulding (earth)

Imagine the space filled with wet clay, and seek to find how the fullness of the body can engage with this substance. How does the body move when embedded in clay?

Attempt to move this substance with the hands, the elbows, the knees. How do you move your physical body to give shape and form to this substance?

You seek to give form to the space you are occupying, which is now filled with wet clay.

Acknowledge that you are coming up against a powerful resistance, since this is wet clay your body is attempting to form.

Your movement will, of necessity, become slower and more determined when it is genuinely seeking to experience what it is to meet strong physical resistance.

Seek to think and feel the body as a movable form, interacting with an earthy substance. Give yourself permission to seek, investigate and discover what this activity is, without asking for results.

It is demanding physically, moving through clay, so pay attention to how to engage the will without resulting in unnecessary muscular tension. Work to bore through the earthy substance with the whole body. Feel what it means to have every inch of the body engaged.

Take your time.

Find how you can enliven and unite inwardly with this outer physical activity.

Every now and then, stop the outer movement and reflect on whether there is an inner response in the realm of sensation or feeling.

Pay attention to whether something is stirring in your feeling life. Is there a perceptible inner response?

Try letting go of the outer physical movement. Walk through the space, carrying within you what has been the inner response. What may have been stirred inwardly by the outward physical activity?

Perhaps you experience what it is to have greater strength and determination in meeting obstacles in life. It may even illuminate a moment of great significance, such as receiving news of a tragic nature.

It is even possible that a character will present itself: for example, a bully character who constantly asserts themselves, pushing all others aside. Or the character could be one who thoroughly enjoys and appreciates the experience of the sensuality of the body. It could be an acclaimed leader who uses their power for benevolent purposes.

Does your inner response differ from the way you usually experience yourself?

Has an emotional response been awakened, which is both known and unknown to you?

The power and strength in the lower half of the body are very active in supporting the upper half of the body. Try letting the arms go and attempt moulding only with the lower half of the body.

It is possible to awaken an inner response to the full-bodied outer activity.

Floating (water)

Imagine the space filled with water. Experience that it is lighter than the earthy wet clay we just experimented with.

See if you can have a sense of being lifted, supported, carried. How does the body respond and move in this watery element?

Imagine being seaweed, anchored to the bottom of the ocean, being played by the water surrounding it. Find, with the greatest of ease, how the watery substance supports this ease.

Lift the arms to the horizontal and rest them on the water. Does a sensation arise?

Perhaps the response is one of experiencing calm and poise. Is your bodily response different from what it was when you were forming wet clay, where resistance was vital?

Notice how one movement can flow into another; that the movement never stops.

Give yourself permission to inwardly relinquish control of your movements, and allow the imagination of water to play your body; converse with your body. The head floats above the neck; the shoulders and arms float above the hips.

Perhaps in your inner being, you can imagine and sense bubbles rising. Let go of the outer movement occasionally. Listen to your inner life, and sense what may be stirred.

The task is to avoid pretending you are moving through the water; avoid performing an idea of it. Seek a genuine experience, a bodily sensation of floating. Seek to unite the outer physical movement with the inner feeling life, so that they become one.

Try imagining a centre above the head. See if this can enable you to sense lifting from the heaviness of earth. This can be used to create a character: for example, Yelena in *Uncle Vanya*. She's sexy, her whole body is sensual, and she floats.

Flying (air)

We are moving from earth to water to air. The imaginative substance is getting lighter.

Can you imagine your body flying through space, where there is no resistance?

Try moving an arm quickly, lightly, easily into the space, away from the body. Sense the release. Seek to let go of controlling the movement.

Experience the opportunity and desire to overcome the weight of your body, the pull of gravity.

Imagine the body filled with air. Imagine your bones are hollow, perhaps filled with blue sky, or that you are a bird perched on a limb ready to take flight.

Allow your imagination to become active and influence how you move.

Imagine a gentle breeze lifting you. Can you find a sense of a joyful lightness and ease beginning to be awakened?

Continue to investigate this possibility with tremendous ease, acknowledging that the body can overcome the weight of the earth. Trust that the outer manifestation of the movement will begin to awaken an inner movement, an inner response: of flying.

Let go of the outer movement at times, and sense what has been awakened inwardly. Can you sustain this sensation? See if you can fly inwardly. There are degrees of flying. It can be controlled, or it can be experienced as total abandonment.

This could inform a character: sanguine, easily moving from one task to another or one thought to another.

Imagine being the actor/dancer Fred Astaire, who never appears to be on the earth: the lightness, the ease, the freedom of movement.

Flying could also inform a moment of great urgency in a play, where a character seeks to escape being seen or caught.

Explore an imaginary centre that is in the collarbones. Sense these bones as wings that will lift you off the earth, giving you a feeling of being weightless.

Radiating (fire)

Close your eyes and imagine flying into the sun. Give yourself time to truly feel this. Allow the bony substance of the physical body to be dissolved, and notice what that sensation is. Seek to become at one with the light and warmth of the sun.

Your physical body and your inner being are at one with the sun.

Give yourself time to feel this possibility. How do you move if your movements are leaping tongues of fire? Find out how this sensation could inform a character. Allow the fire to resolve into radiating light.

Now experiment with radiating in all directions. Sense the light radiating off the surface of the body, the back of the hands, the palms of the hands.

Can you imagine the bones and muscles dissolving into pure light?

Who could this be? Does it broaden your scope of what's possible?

You are seeking to experience the body as being permeated with light, sensing that you are a body of total bright light.

How do you move when you are sending streaks of light into the space around you?

Can you sense that you are at one with the light? You are filled with the generosity of giving, perhaps becoming the room's light source: radiating light, shedding light, sharing light.

Entertain the possibility of experiencing a deep, penetrating warmth. Nothing is lighter than light. Throughout your exploration, note that your movement makes your inner life available to you, allowing it to participate fully.

Listen to your movement and see if you can sense that the outer movement is constantly playing back on your inner life.

Moulding, floating, flying and radiating

After you have acquired an experience of each of the qualities separately, try metamorphosing from radiating to flying to floating to moulding.

See if you can go from one quality to the other and experience what lies between them. This metamorphosis can go both ways: either heaviest to lightest or lightest to heaviest.

Experiment with being moulded by the earth, floated by the water, flown by air, radiated by the sun's light.

What did moulding elicit? Determination? power? What about floating – was it calm, spacy? What was flying – was it excitement, or joy? With radiating, was there confidence or courage?

Qualities of movement – advanced

Exercise 1

Find out how easy you can be with yourself: sense your body in movement and allow yourself to luxuriate in movement.

Engage the space. Swim in it. Be awake to your relationship to space in all six directions.

How can you engage the fullness of your body with the fullness of space?

Allow the space to feed you; you don't have to work the body's physicality so much. Let the body be moved by the space; the space itself begins to mould you.

You are at the centre of the activity; at the same time, you are being played by the space.

Know the space is filled with moulding. There is no escaping moulding in this space. That is what is happening. You are being moulded. Seek to enter into that activity, that imagination.

Sense the activity of moulding living in and around you.

The process remains the same as you continue floating, flying and radiating.

You are receptive to the space. You receive the quality from the space, and allow the space to move you. The space does the work for you. Can you discover something about these qualities when you allow the space to provide you with the activity?

Exercise 2

Seek to engage in the activity of moulding, floating, flying, radiating, by first establishing a quality/sensation along with an imaginary centre.

Begin moving confidently. Add precision to the confidence. Enliven the centre in the belly, create exact forms into the space, and find yourself moulding.

Begin moving gently and quietly with ease, with an imaginary centre above the head, and find your way into floating.

Move playfully, lightly, quickly, mischievously, with an imaginary centre in the collarbones as if they were wings, and move into flying.

Move with courage, generosity, and gallantry, with an imaginary centre in the chest, and find your way into radiating.

Exercise 3

Establish the activity of moulding, floating, flying, radiating, each as a separate quality, into the four corners of the room.

Move from one to the other in any combination.

It could be radiating to floating, flying to moulding.

Find your own way. Stay with each.

Enter into the activity in each corner, and track your journey between one quality to another. Pay special attention to in between: the transition from one to the other. Track your process.

Four brothers – a beginner's class

Let's find a feeling of ease with our bodies.

Move the hands through space as if washing them in warm water, bringing the arms into play, easily. The arms will carry the entire torso into this flowing, effortless movement.

Let's find that which Chekhov refers to as 'a feeling of ease' as the torso joins the lower half of the body: the hips, the legs, the feet.

We are seeking full-bodied participation. We are allowing this new unity of the upper and lower half of the body to add life, strength and ease to the fullness of your movement. Repeat to yourself inwardly, 'Easily, go easily'.

Find it in your spine, elbows and joints – until, ultimately, you experience it as an inner reality.

Move about the room with a sense of lightness and ease.

Now, pick up a chair, bring it across the room and set it down. As you do so, find out how you move with that chair. You can always find ease, regardless of the obstacle. In this case, the obstacle is the chair. So, how do you move the chair with ease?

Pick up an imaginary baby – or a wounded bird – with a complete sense of ease.

From a simple standing position, begin to feel the body as slightly heavier than usual.

Now sink into a chair.

Give your weight to it, sensing it with your back, your bottom and the back of your legs. Sense the shape and form of the chair you are giving your weight to.

The chair has a back that is touching your back. It has four legs and the flat surface you are resting on. Sense this form and solidity. Picture it.

The chair holds you with its form.

Now slowly rise to a standing position. You've separated your form from the form of the chair.

Sense your uprightness, the straight line of your spine, your legs, your arms at your side, your ten fingers and the space between them.

Sense the flatness of the soles of your feet as they contact the solid floor.

Now break those straight lines of arms, legs, spine, as you discover and sense that this form, unlike the chair, is a movable form. You create straight and curved lines in your movement through space.

Pick up the chair with your hands on either side of the back. Lift it, set it down, and tilt it. Let this contact with a solid object give you a greater sense of form.

A feeling – a sense of form – is what we are seeking.

We are moving about the room, sitting, kneeling, etc.

All activities have a beginning, a middle and an end. This sense, however, does not result in rigidity. And to ensure that it doesn't, begin to allow ease to arise of its own into your movements.

The ease does not replace this sense of form – it joins the form.

Can you now begin to sense that ease and form are occupying the same space through your physicality, joining together in one energy unit?

One element doesn't dominate the other; they move together in harmony.

Stay with that marriage of the two – ease and form. You may then begin to realize that the union of these two creates a living reality of beauty.

On the stage, even a simple act, like taking a picture of a loved one off a table or a mantelpiece, creates a moment of quiet beauty; even a moment of violence on stage must create an artistic picture of beauty.

Now I ask you on your own to revisit these three elements of Chekhov's four brothers – ease, form, beauty.

Find some space for yourself where you can move freely.

In an upright position, close your eyes and visualize yourself making a strong, full-bodied movement or gesture.

Open your eyes and execute that movement as fully as you pictured it. Repeat this several times – precede each with the mental picture of what you are attempting to do, then do it.

Let's break that movement down into three segments: beginning, middle, end.

Before executing the gesture, be very conscious of exactly when the engagement of that movement begins, holding a picture of it before you move.

Then make the movement, and then, having completed it, feel the whole cycle coming to its end.

Now begin working once again with ease. Add form and beauty, one at a time, noticing how each addition adds a fuller sensation towards a sense of wholeness.

Four brothers – advanced

Having a sense of the fullness of your physical form, begin moving just the upper portions of your body – the lower half, hips, legs and feet are fixed to the floor.

Find ease with the hands, arms, shoulders, torso: a fluid movement of ease in all the muscles surrounding the spine.

Lift the arms with the image and knowledge that the hands follow the direction of the arms, then let the hands lead the arms and shoulders until the entire torso is moving with a sense of ease.

As the upper half begins to engage the hips, lower back, thighs, calves, heels, balls of the feet and torso, allow this new unity of upper and lower half to add life and strength to the fullness of your movement. Make forms in the space you're moving in.

This new sense of form you're moving with releases a stronger sense and power of ease.

The muscles are infused with that sense of ease, while the bones – the skeleton, give a strong sense of form.

Two elements are now married in one physical form – ease and form. Take your time, going from one to the other. Ease to form, form to ease, until the movement itself unites the two as one unit of energy.

As the space opens up to your movement, allow a greater sense of fullness. Be alert to the presence of a sense of beauty as it comes of its own accord.

Perhaps the movement itself and the sense of spaciousness surrounding you will call forth a quiet presence of beauty. Beauty arises out of the marriage of the two, a sense of ease and form together.

What will then arise in your working for a time with these separate elements?

Radiating and receiving

Exercise 1

Find a partner and begin passing a ball between you.

This can be an unconscious, habitual bodily response to a suggestion, requiring little conscious activity.

Begin to engage consciously with giving the ball and taking what is given.

Be awake to what happens with how you throw the ball once you've given it to your partner, wanting them to receive it as if you're offering a gift.

Follow inwardly the movement of the ball as it travels the distance between you.

Sense movement going away from you, towards your partner.

Contact the centre in the chest and sense that your arms come out of that centre, not the shoulder.

Choose to release the ball from the actor's ideal centre into the space between. You are wanting to connect and contact another.

This activity sends out and puts substance into the space between you and your partner.

Does a gesture suggest itself? That of expressing, giving generously into the front-space? Sense the possibility of the gesture originating in the back-space.

Take your time.

What is asked of you is to be open and available to take in what is given, to create an inner space within, from which you can genuinely receive.

Seek the gesture that will support you in this endeavour. Trust the body to reveal the gesture, when it is given the suggestion: to open and be awake to what is given.

Find how it is possible to open into the back-space, which will strengthen your ability to continue taking in and receiving.

Give yourself sufficient time to explore.

Stay with the exercise for some time, always seeking and connecting to what these two activities are.

How do they manifest in your feeling life? What's the content each carries?

Sense an invisible stream flowing between you. Perhaps it can be sensed as a golden thread. The drama is not with the giver or the taker; it is in the space between.

You seek to fill the space with substance, which is born through actively connecting with someone or something outside yourself, moving towards giving and opening to receive.

Experiment with changing the distance between you when throwing the ball – close, then far away – maintaining the activity, the connection, the substance created between.

Add words to the exchange. Throw the ball (give) with, 'Here'. Catch the ball (receive) with, 'Thank you'.

Avoid the temptation to be overly social, as this will overshadow the activity you're seeking and take you into a known, habitual way of being with another.

See if you can invite every part of your body to participate.

Become curious about the scope of radiating and receiving, and be gentle with yourself. At the same time, find how to broaden your capacity with these two realms of activity.

Find the outer and inner journey of going from one to the other.

These activities may begin to feel familiar. It may feel that this is something you know and can recognize.

Exercise 2

Let go of the ball and your partner.

Find something in the room that interests you.

Let your attention be drawn out through your interest.

Is there a sense that you are inwardly moving towards that object of interest?

Play with this sense.

Find in yourself the ability to recognize the sensation of movement that fills the space between you and the object.

Let's name this what Michael Chekhov calls 'radiating'.

Seek the sense of inviting an object of interest to come to you, to draw it towards you, being available and open to taking it in, to receiving it.

These activities have a direction of movement: one goes out; one comes in.

Exercise 3

Find a partner.

Ask for permission from each other as to where you will allow your partner to touch you.

One of you will close your eyes and allow yourselves to be touched.

The challenge is to find what it is to be open and receptive to touch, not knowing what part of the body will be touched. This requires trust in one another and it requires being sensitive. It requires being open, available and willing to receive.

Listen to what is asked of you. What is stirred when you are consciously engaging in the activity of receiving?

You are in a safe environment. Perhaps you are challenged in your perception of what it is to receive. Be awake and listen to your response and how your body reacts.

Take turns.

Give each other feedback.

The task is to find out what it is to truly receive.

You may feel it as an inner challenge. Recognize this and be free of judgement. See if you can become interested in it as a phenomenon of being alive.

Exercise 4

Find a partner and stand back to back.

Take a few steps away, then turn and face each other. Your only task is to take in the other. Be receptive to who is in front of you.

How long can you sustain being receptive? Take in their posture, form, clothes, hairstyle and facial features.

Be specific.

You may choose to take a step backward or forward, attempting to create more or less space between you. This will allow you to participate more fully in taking in, to receive what is being presented.

When you choose, you may take a step towards or away from your partner, sending your interest to them. Radiating to them. This could take the form of an inner question. This whole experience could involve engaging the question of 'what is radiating and what am I receiving?'

It could feel like you are penetrating your partner, to understand better what is going on between you.

Different gestures may present themselves, but what you are primarily seeking now is to go out – to radiate – or to take in – to receive.

If it is a mystery that engages you, embrace the mystery and stay curious.

Luxuriate in not having to know. Instead, you're alive, awake, engaged.

Touch and contact

Let's explore the difference between touch and contact.

Let's begin by taking in this room and attempting to rediscover it.

Notice the light. Notice the ceiling, the floor. You might consider the colour of the carpet, the colour of the room, the right angles.

Be here in the space, consciously.

Take your time.

Is there anything about the space you've never noticed?

Now, begin to touch what you see, just lightly, with your fingertips.

The objects, the walls, windows, articles of clothing. Only lightly touch for a moment.

Don't linger with this inquiry: you're just looking for the initial texture sensation.

Now go back to those objects you touched.

Press your hand against an object. Pick it up. Make actual contact with it. Its substance. Is it soft or hard? If it's a chair or smaller object, sense its weight, its texture, its temperature.

It's not the surface you want to notice now – make actual contact with this object, with its substance.

Find a partner and put your hand on their shoulder. Feel that you go beyond the surface of the skin and into them. Grasp their shoulder as if you wish them good luck.

We know these moments of inwardness: for example, when we make physical contact with a friend. Perhaps it's only a handshake, or holding their hand with both of yours. At these moments, something of ourselves releases into the other. It's either a gift or an intrusion, but it is a genuine activity.

Now let's form a circle and throw the ball.

With the ball in your hand, come into an inner readiness to throw it to someone.

Look downwards at the floor. Decide who you will throw the ball to, then lift your head and look at that person.

Let that moment of contact arrive. You are looking at another 'I'; another ego is looking back at you. Let this moment in, while staying alert to that inner reality of seeing and allowing yourself to be seen by another I.

Allow that reality to exist, resisting any personal need to be social, pleasant or friendly – which is most often an act of self-protection.

Our aim here is to be available to the other and throw the ball on that stream of contact, on that stream of presence.

Now let's walk out of the circle, out of that concentration. Let's be free of it, breathe it out.

Free the body – the neck, shoulders and back.

As you walk, have the image that your arms come right out of the centre in the chest. The legs are cut up to that centre. There is no tension to staunch your action. Put breath into your movement.

Now, once again, let's make ourselves present to ourselves.

The three centres

Let's allow the lower half of the body to make itself known and available to us – that physical centre in the stomach. That life down there, that energy, is a physical reality of *vitality*.

It's happy to be acknowledged.

Sense it, be with it; let that vitality fill the lower half of the body until it becomes like a stallion that carries the upper part of the body through the space.

Explore a sense of power, non-aggressive power, life, vitality. Give yourself time to play, to investigate, to explore.

Now put your attention on the head, the highest physical centre. Give it the quality of *wakefulness*; clear-headed is what we are after.

We are awake – as if we plunged our heads into a cold mountain stream.

Look out from there into the world. Notice elements of the room you're in that you haven't seen before.

Now you can see, hear and make decisions and judgements, and through this area of your being, you can be present in a different way.

You are a two-fold being.

The great energy from below, in your will centre, wants to give life to your fingertips, to the soles of your feet, to the space between your fingers. This joins with the wakefulness and clarity of the head centre.

Let these two areas vibrate. Stay with this sense of two-foldness for some time.

Observe how this clarity and energy – this vitality and wakefulness – abide with each other.

At some point, there may awaken in you a sense of something lacking – a middle that we need to complete.

Right there, in the middle between the two, is the centre of the chest.

We point to there when we say 'I' or 'me'. 'I want'. 'Are you talking to me?' I. That is yours. That is where you meet the world, join the world, go out to the world: to that which interests you, that which you love.

Chekhov calls this centre the actor's ideal centre. Walk with it now. Be with it. Carry it. How deep does it go?

It is there inside you, between the belly and the head. If you locate your lower centre through a feeling of warmth, and the head centre through a sense of clarity, light and wakefulness, this ideal centre you can find through an open gesture. Open that place, that location. This is a centre for *opening*. You endow it with the warmth from the belly and the light from the head. They meet there in the middle.

The sun in the chest is the image for that centre. Now walk with this image. Carry it inside yourself. It will soon cease to be just a picture.

Everyone knows how to be generous with their friends, with other people. Be generous now with yourself. Let this centre abide in you, in your chest: a centre of warmth and light.

This is where impulses make themselves known, where the will becomes conscious and moves outwards.

This centre is life in the chest. The actor's heart; the actor's ideal centre. This ideal centre doesn't realize itself until it is coupled with a periphery. Centre and periphery at once, at the same time.

Let's use the room you're in as your periphery. As an inner gesture, move out to the walls of the room. Expand the energy of your centre to the circumference or perimeter of the room you are in, then, perhaps, beyond. Keep the source of that energy there in the chest.

As if in answer to the question, 'Where are you?' point to the periphery with a finger of one hand and point to the middle of your chest with a finger of the other hand, at the same time. Say 'I am here'. That's centre and periphery; that is called presence.

You carry centre and periphery with you as you move around the room.

In feeling these three centres and this newfound presence, you begin to feel the fullness of the physical body: its form and shape. You are feeling in movement that this fully present physical form is one unit of energy.

Feel your weight with the soles of the feet as you move forward. Feel the lengthening of the spine, the movement of your arms, the space between your fingers, the shape of the hands.

Using the sense of your movement, you have freed yourself from your body's learned resistance. Can you sense now that there is no unwanted tension in the shoulders, neck or back?

There can begin to appear a sense of wholeness to the physical form: a sense of your movement as one unit of energy. You fill the space with your free movement using the widest space possible.

Your whole, free, physical form is now in readiness to explore Chekhov's exercises.

Directions[2]

There are six 'primary colours' of directions: front, back, in, out, up, down. These contain millions of experiences. It's not true to say that one is positive and another negative.

In working with directions, remember always to take the crucial final step: give the experience over entirely to the inner life. Let the body be easy, and let the inner life take over. Give yourself some space for this process to settle within, and feel how the experience gets stronger once it works on our innermost selves. That is where it really effects change or transformation.

Maybe you test out a piece of text on this inner experience. As a musician might practise their scales, perhaps you test out a monologue in all six directions.

If you have trouble experiencing one direction, notice how it is different from another direction. Sometimes by comparing or seeing what it is not, we discover more of what it *is*.

Direction is psycho-physical. This first exercise is about experiencing the potential of the psychological value of direction. To get the actor into their sense of direction is the first step, so we can get them into their sense of action.

Front

Stand in a room facing a wall, be at some distance from the wall.

Imagine your body is filled with arrows, from the bottom of the feet to the top of the head. These arrows carry your interest and attention.

Aim these arrows forward, towards the wall ahead of you.

---

[2]The transcripts in this section are from classes with Bethany Caputo.

Be aware right away of the shift – and listen to what comes to meet you. Perhaps anxiety wakes up, perhaps eagerness, perhaps ambition. Listen for a tempo that begins to make itself known. Listen for energy in the will, and begin to detect what this front-space makes you want to do.

Now take a step towards the wall. That is to say, take a step in the direction the inner life is going and let the body follow that inner life.

Take another step. And another.

Feel this forward energy; this front-space life increases with each step.

Now, take a step backward, but keep the inner life going forward.

The arrows are still shooting out towards the wall ahead of you, through the shins and the stomach, from your back to your front.

Now, turn and face another wall. Same thing.

Walk towards the wall and away. All the while, it's as if those arrows of attention and interest draw the entirety of you forward. You desire to enter into the wall itself, perhaps penetrating through it and beyond.

Life begins to happen one hundred per cent in front of you. It's as if life begins at the body and goes forward.

Turn to another wall, and another, and now to no wall but to the room.

You have activated the front-space. Go out into it.

What is this waking up? Is it familiar? Is it circumstantial? Is this you on a good day? Is this you on a busy street in a busy city? Is this you when you are late to work? Is there a whiff of another facet of you in this forward experience, or do you feel like someone else completely is emerging?

We are not aiming for a character. We haven't even started acting yet. We are only curious about what the front-space wakes up in us. But if a character – or the hint of a character or personality or tendency – comes to meet us, so be it.

What part of you is this?

Take a slight pause here.

Now, give this experience over entirely to the inner life. So, outwardly, it may not be altogether evident that you are working with the front-space, but energetically, inwardly, the experience that is working on you is completely forward.

Do some pedestrian things: sit down, stand up, fold a blanket, get a sip of water. What is this new reality? What is this experience?

Maybe test out some text in this experience. Do not bend the experience to make sense of the text; let the experience bend the text.

Ask yourself: What does one hundred per cent forward wake up in you? What is the psychological value of this experience of front-space?

Back

Repeat this exercise for the back-space.

This time, be in the room with the wall now behind you, be at some distance from the wall.

Imagine your body is filled with arrows, from the bottom of the feet to the top of the head. These arrows carry your interest and attention.

Aim these arrows backward, towards the wall behind you. Be aware right away of the shift – and listen to what comes to meet you.

Listen for a tempo that begins to make itself known. Listen for energy, and begin to detect what this back-space makes you want to do.

Now take a step backward towards the wall that is behind you. Take a step in the direction the inner life is going, and let the body follow that inner life.

Take another step. And another.

Feel this backward energy; this back-space life increases with each step.

Now, take a step forward, but keep the inner life going backward.

The arrows are still shooting out to the wall behind you, through the shins and the stomach, from your front to your back.

Now, turn and face another wall. Same thing.

Walk towards the wall and away. All the while, it's as if those arrows of attention and interest draw 100 per cent of you backward.

Turn to another wall, and another, and now to no wall but to the room.

You have activated the back-space.

Be aware that when it comes time to move forward into the room holding this, the imagination has a little more to do to keep the attention going backward, because we walk forward in life. As you walk forward, keep your attention on the movement of the inner life going backward. It will feel very natural after a time, when you find your way with it.

Never forget to take the most crucial step: to give the experience over to the inner life. There is a time in discovery for bold and obvious action – almost 'overacting' – and there is a time to let that initial exploration subside and seek a more integrated experience. There is a settling that happens then, where you let all the sensation you gained from boldly exploring the image/movement inform your inner life. To let the experience affect us at our core is to have the experience influence us the most. If you can allow an experience to exist on the level of your soul, then the rest of you is available to be present to the moment, while the experience works on and in you.

Once you have been through this exercise completely, you can do it relatively efficiently by simply reactivating the front- and back-space. Stand in one spot and lean forward towards your toes to the front, without falling over, to wake up the front-space. Then lean to the back, towards the heels, without falling over, to activate the back-space.

In and out

What I outline here is a precursor to expanding and contracting. In and out directions can be seen as related to expanding and contracting but different altogether.

I encourage you to think of this exercise in terms of introverted and extroverted – not the personality types, but where the direction of your attention is. When you go in, it's because your attention is drawn inwards. When you go out, it's because your attention is pulled outward.

Take the arrows we worked with earlier, and aim them inwards.

Dive right into the middle of your centre: the arrows turn in on themselves and go right to your core. This requires imagination and concentration, at first. After a while, the sensation will be all you need to have this inward experience.

Try to focus on the directional experience. We don't land anywhere; we are in a constant state of moving. Our attention is on movement. Our energy is moving in a direction, and that direction is inward.

Go for a test drive around the room. What is life like when your attention is inwards?

Try some of the same things you did before. Fluff a pillow; fold a blanket; look for something in the room you lost; get a sip of water. Ask yourself what wakes up in you when your focus is inwards.

What do you notice? What draws your attention? Are you social or not?

What is the psychological value of this simple and everyday experience of turning inwards? Does another experience rise to meet this one? Is there an image within you?

Do you feel a sense of sadness? Or a protectiveness? Is it a retreat to your happy place or a calm inner peacefulness?

There doesn't have to be a concrete sense of experience; it is enough to experience that you are sending your attention and interest inwards. Sometimes things come to meet our experience, and it is our business to simply notice them.

Is this a calming place, a sad place, a closed-off place, a fearful sensation? Is it a retreat, a contemplating? Does it give rise to strength, to a sense of silence and/or listening?

What comes to meet you will be different every time you send your energy in a direction, just as any exercise done repeatedly will yield different results each time.

Now, send those arrows *out* from you.

This is different from forward; this is out in all directions. Can you send your energy out, waking up the directional tendency outwards, and still keep your centre within you?

Repeat the same pedestrian activities, noticing all the while: What is this experience? Who is this person? Is it me at certain times, or not me at all? Is this circumstantial?

Does it wake up my senses to something dangerous? Or is it an experience of pure elation or joy?

These exercises are not meant to be the end of the line. Rather, they are the beginning of sensing the psycho-physical.

If you can sense yourself in direction, you can sense the psychological value of that direction. You are then on your way to sensing more complex experiences, like gestures.

Direction is a fundamental first step in any action. Do you want to go towards someone or away from them? Do you grow in the presence of this person, or in these circumstances, or do you shrink?

If you can sense this, and if your body can answer it for you, then you are on your way to sensing something more nuanced, like what the body wants to do as it moves outward: to discover, to enlighten, to illuminate or to break open, for example.

Down

Borrowing from the law of gravity, raise an arm up and let it drop down. Raise your other arm. Let it drop down. Seek the sensation of gravity, which is down.

As safely as you can, let the whole body drop straight down. Feel the weight of yourself as that weight relates to the pull of gravity.

They say every step is a stopped fall. Can you take a slow step and feel the gravity in this action – the frequent and straightforward action of stepping?

Lean against a wall, almost ready to slide down it, and feel the pull of gravity. Slide down the wall now and feel the insistence of that pull.

Try not to get stuck on the floor with this exercise. Once we are on the floor, the movement and, therefore, the sensation stops.

Now begin to walk around the room with the sensation of down alive around you, and slowly make your way to simple activities: fold a blanket, fluff a pillow, move something from one side of the room to the next, find something you lost in the room or get ready to leave the house.

Little by little, this becomes more of an inner activity, and the sensation of down stays alive within you. Outwardly, your movements become more pedestrian, more 'natural', but inwardly, the sensation of down is active, and your psychology is adjusted.

What is this experience? Who is this person? Is this you in a specific circumstance? Is this you when you have received some negative news? Or is this you when you feel grounded and strong?

The experience becomes an inner experience, and like with every task in the Chekhov work, there is a glorious spot at which it becomes an inner truth, when the body has done all the work it needs and is now simply receptive to the experience within. The experience gets stronger, and it radiates back out from us.

Look out from yourself. Feel this experience of down ripple out from you. Feel that you don't need to do anything more to generate it; it is working on you and in you, and you now simply have the privileged task to feel that and notice your surroundings and ask yourself what it makes you want to do (the final question in any element of the technique).

Up

Just as there is gravity, there is levity. Start by just saying the word 'up'. Repeat it. 'Up'. It's light and straight up.

Imagine you are a marionette, with strings attached to your wrists and one ankle. Let those strings gently draw those three points up, and then repeat that with the other leg.

We are trying to get a pure experience of up before making it a psycho-physical exploration.

Now imagine this levity as a gentler force, lifting you up off the earth, into the upright and beyond. Gently roll forward down the spine. As you unroll into your upright position, let the final unravel be the point that launches you into this experience of up. One hundred per cent up.

What comes to meet you in up? Take it for a test drive around the room.

What is life like in up? Who is this person? Is this you after you receive favourable news? Is this an experience of wonder?

Before you nail it down as this or that, keep discovering it.

There are millions of possibilities, and it will be different each time you come to it. For now, discover what has come to meet you today.

Are you rising up out of anger or disbelief? Or does this experience of up lighten your load? Is it slightly – or totally – blissful?

Do some pedestrian activities and see how life is slightly different with this experience of up.

Trajectories

Pick one trajectory: front and back; up and down; or out and in. Try one monologue all the way through, and go between the two poles, inwardly, of course. You might move slowly or quickly from the front-space to the back-space. You might perhaps make a few stops along the trajectory of forward and backward, just for discovery.

Transformative tools

Imaginary centres

Think of our three physical centres: the will, the head, the chest. Their location, quality and primary activity. Return to the centre in the chest now, and sense its light and warmth, its ability to open.

Let's engage our imaginations, uniting an image with that specific location in the body. Now keep the location the same, in the chest, but seek to change the *quality*.

First, allowing that centre in the chest to become *cold and dark*. This is the centre of your being; it defines you. Give your attention entirely to that imaginary centre. Feel that you look out into the world from that dark, cold centre. It does your seeing for you. Draw and concentrate your whole being to this one location and let it work on you.

What does it mean for this to be the centre of your being?

Be patient in finding your way into focusing and concentrating your attention on this particular location, with these specific qualities. If you find yourself too inwardly engaged, seek to connect more fully with movement.

Focus your attention entirely on that centre and allow it to inform you: how it invites you to move, in what direction and in what tempo. Take time here.

Be willing not to know where this is leading you; to welcome the unknown.

Eventually, you may sense you are met with a suggestion of someone who is not your everyday experience of yourself. Who is it that comes to meet you?

Find the inner reality and listen to what is awakened in your feeling life.

How does the imaginary centre affect your physical body and its movements? Are they deliberate or casual? Quick or slow?

Be awake to the new things that come to you. Respect the inner struggle to stay with the image and manifest it as a reality.

You are not expected to show or act anything. Permit yourself to engage with the imagination fully.

Sense what it is to be you now. What has been brought to life through living in this particular part of the body, with this particular quality? How do you walk, hold your hands, respond to the front- and back-space?

See if you can change the quality of the centre in the chest again to *being empty, hollowed out*. It's a significant change.

Allow that imagination to work upon you, and listen to the effect that it may bring about. What effect does it have on how you experience who you are?

Does it call forth a sensation that is familiar to you, or is it an unknown experience? Listen to the sensation that has arisen.

After fully taking in the experience, and acknowledging the sensation that may have arisen, let it go.

Now, locate *the sense of your spine*. Give yourself time to do this. Once you sense your spine, imagine it cold and made of steel. Appeal to your imagination to enable you to experience that as a reality.

We are seeking to increase our power to express multiple possibilities.

Be open to exploring how this affects your movement, your relation to space, your relation to other people. Consider the possibility that imaginary centres enable you to remove a limited conception of yourself.

Stay with what has been awakened in you, and absorb whatever the experience has been.

Then, freely release the image and walk away from it and back to your centre in the chest: back to the known experience of what it is to be you.

Straight lines and curves with imaginary centres

We'll start with a passage from *To the Actor*.

> Now let us try to distinguish between the character as a whole and the characterization, which can be defined as a small, peculiar feature of the character. A characterization or peculiar feature can be anything indigenous to the character: a typical movement, a characteristic manner of speech, a recurrent habit, a certain way of laughing, walking or wearing a suit, an odd way of holding the hands. . . . These small peculiarities are a kind of finishing touches which an artist bestows upon his creation. The whole character seems to become more alive, more human and true, as soon as it is endowed with such a peculiar little feature.[3]

We tend to be afraid of these 'small, peculiarities' – slight tics, certain mannerisms – in rehearsals. You have to be brave to try it.

Characteristics or mannerisms go through many stages. Don't constantly be saying, 'Is this real? Is this believable?' Just try it. Of course, it's going to feel stuck on at some point. But then it moves. It moves into something else.

Let's begin to work with a straight line and a curved line, very lightly.

What we want to do to start is to get a psycho-physical sensation of a *straight* line. Anything that is an angle with the body. Find what is straight with your physical form. Our arms are straight, our legs are straight. We might simply be drawing a straight line in space.

Spend some time with this. Don't rush. Investigate.

---

[3] *To the Actor*, 82–3.

Then, in contrast, explore a sense of *curved*. I can do it with my hands. All of these places that break, I can sense that my body is a curve. Watch dancers; they are brilliant at making curves.

Now, just for the moment, pick one or the other. Either straight line *or* curve.

What you want to do is somehow bring the physical reality of that into a psychological reality.

Take it inside, naturally.

If you choose straight, this doesn't mean that you will be a stick. Let's just say that the straight line has a very bright centre in the head. With the curved line, you will add a very soft, warm centre in the belly. There is something like pizza dough somewhere in the belly. It's warm. Your relationship with the earth is different than it would be if the centre was in the head.

Then go back to broad movements with either curved or straight lines.

When you take it inwardly, ask yourself who this is. Don't start acting it. Ask yourself, 'What is my relationship to my physical body?' Bring it a little more into your feeling life: this curve or this straight line. Allow it to lead you someplace. Just listen to it.

Continue to work. To explore. Ask 'how do I use my hands?', for example.

Something in your actor's being is responding to straight, or curved, though you're not displaying it or demonstrating that. It's your actor's secret.

Right now, you are just testing the waters with your fingertips. Tasting it. Exploring it.

Don't make up your mind too fast about what exactly it is. It can be a lot of things. Straight lines can be helpful or arrogant. Imagining a clear, bright centre in the head will also lend suggestions.

You can use text, but not for too long – just to test it out. To see what's there. Because you are asking yourself, 'Who is this?', you may have an immediate response to it.

Then go back to the physicality. What are the feet like of someone who is a curved line? What are the feet like of somebody who is a straight line?

What are the mannerisms of this person?

Working around your two definite choices is the centre – the belly or the head.

How do you walk? How do you hold the head?

Do the hands tend to be soft, even sloppy? Or very formed?

In terms of the voice, does this person live more in the vowels? Or the consonants?

Then go back to the idea of straight lines or curved lines. Go back to the primary thing: is this person a straight line or curve? Just deepen that idea a little. Live with it so that it is singular. Get more in touch with the psycho-physical. A straight line is a very different sensation than a curved line. What's this person's ability or non-ability to go out to others?

You can also ask yourself, 'What is the pure inner experience of a straight line or curve?'

As you bring it inward, let it speak to you; don't guide it. You are working with that one choice.

At some point, you can add the centre's location without the quality, then add the quality.

This is just an opportunity to explore the term 'psycho-physical'. Inner and outer, at the same time.

Now let's play with a new suggestion: the centre for the straight line is still the head, but it's *very dark*. No light goes out; no light comes in. See what happens. Don't figure it out.

If you chose curved, the centre is still the stomach, but the quality is *hard and cold*, not warm and soft.

I have just changed the qualities, not the location of the centre.

See how all these different choices can affect you – not how you affect them. What is your relationship to those choices?

What of their physical appearance? How do others see them?

Now, let's explore a change of centre.

If you chose straight, the centre is now outside the head, moving all around the head. It constantly moves.

If you chose curved, the centre in the belly moves outside, to right under the butt. It's heavy, pulling you down a little, right under the rear end.

The degree of heaviness is up to you: find the degree of heaviness that you can live with. The heaviness is outside; it's as though it's hanging there.

Let it do the work for you.

If this suggests certain mannerisms, try them out.

Finally, just let everything vanish into thin air, except straight or curved lines.

You can go back to some movement, but make the activity minimal. Stay with that one idea: straight line or curved line. It becomes more psycho than physical. More inner than outer.

Just stop for a moment, take a couple of deep breaths, and walk out.

Staccato and legato

In this exercise, look for something going out. Are you sending it out from the chest centre, down through the shoulders and arms, and out the windows of the fingertips? What is it to send something out beyond the fingertips? Can you go beyond the walls of the room? Can you send your attention, energy, focus and forces in those different directions?

In staccato and legato's purest form, you get a sense that whatever movement you make strongly has an echo to it. With both of your arms and hands and your fingers pointed in one direction, it's much easier to sense that something leaves you and goes out into space.

There are six directions of space: right, left, up, down, front, back. Bring these directions into consciousness by freely moving the whole body into each direction, loosely and with ease.

Sense the difference, although it may be subtle, between right and left, up and down, front and back.

Standing upright and in place, fling or thrust an arm out to the right, point and say, 'Look!' Seek to go beyond the fingertips into the space, participating fully in the movement as it goes out from you.

Repeat this activity in all six directions. Find how the fullness of the body participates in this movement. Allow the body to turn and lean into the movement.

Let the movement be quick and light, staccato. Let it have the quality of lightning.

'Look' is often something we say when we want someone to see something far away. With this exercise, we seek to open to the space, recognize, and make available the vast dimensions of space.

Now that you have done it with one arm, do the same with both arms.

Seek a strong sense of form that will allow the arms to come out of the ideal centre in a horizontal line, extending through the fingertips.

By necessity, the entire body is alert, awake, engaged.

Return to the centre between each direction, with the body upright. Sense being at home, upright and awake to the ideal centre before moving into each direction.

There is a rhythmic sequence to the movements: right, return, left, return, up, return, down, return, front, return, back, return. Each time you return from a given direction, become centred in the upright. Gather yourself to give fully into the next direction. This requires being intensely awake, in readiness, available to strong directional movement. Find how to be centred in stillness and then actively engaged in intense movement in different directions. Be aware that the impulse for movement in each direction may initiate an inner movement that precedes the outer. This is part of the preparation.

Now, inwardly, prepare to go into the six directions with a flowing legato movement, similar to that of a river. Sense a feeling of pouring into each direction, into the space, beyond the fingertips.

When moving upward, seek to allow your movement to continue and reach the stars. When moving downward, seek to allow your movement to continue and reach into the earth's centre. When going to the right and left, and front and back, go beyond the boundaries of the walls, into the street, into the woods.

This requires being alert, fully awake, available, in readiness, going out and returning to home base. You're extending beyond the boundaries set by the physical form, getting acquainted with space, bringing it to consciousness.

Repeat, repeat, repeat. It can be of value to repeat all six directions in a set and repeat that set several times, testing out each quality throughout.

Keep questioning what it means to release and open into the space, and make it available. Seek to maintain your curiosity and interest in the nature and intention of this exercise.

Your bodily movement is not as important as your desire to give out everything. Continue to find what that experience is.

All the while, you are seeking to continue to build on the experience of staccato and legato. You are asking the whole of you what wakes up within you with the different experiences of staccato and legato.

Loosen the body between the staccato and legato movements. Shake out and soften the body; regain ease and readiness.

When you feel comfortable with the form individually, listen to one another as an ensemble to find a common impulse for each movement. Be open and available to allow the whole of the group to strengthen your experience.

Now, move into the space with full-bodied staccato movements. Imagine you're engaging musically with the entire body in your movement.

Touch an object and immediately change from light and quick movements to slow, flowing legato movements. Find the dynamic in the change of moving from one quality to another.

Relate to another actor or actors and allow the change to be born out of contact with them. Let go of the outer movements and experience each as an inner sensation.

Move back and forth between the outer movements and sensing an inner content as a result of the movement.

Bring these qualities into speaking a few lines of text. Allow the speech to ride on the activity.

Perhaps each quality can inform you of something in your text that you hadn't realized was there.

Qualities of movement with tempo

Let's start easily with moulding, beginning only with the hands – the heel of the hands, the palms, the fingertips. Each part of the hand will give you a different sensation of moulding.

Gradually find this quality of movement with the whole hand, and even with the space between the fingers.

We are using this quality of movement – moulding – to give us back the fullness of our bodies.

Begin to include the arms with the hands, then the torso with the arms, then the lower half of the body with the torso, until you feel the body as one unit of energy.

Now begin the journey through all four qualities: moulding, floating, flying, radiating.

Work primarily with that space between each – moulding into floating, floating into flying, flying into radiating – where floating still has a bit of moulding in it, where flying still has a bit of floating in it, where radiating still has a bit of flying in it, before becoming a full-bodied experience.

You are metamorphosing one quality into another. And, in doing so, you are giving yourself the experience of going from the heaviest – moulding – to the lightest – radiating.

This activity of transformation is your focus and intention. Each movement has the quality of flowing, one into the other.

Give yourself plenty of time for working through all four, and then perhaps go back from radiating to moulding.

You may now want to work with only two qualities of movement: moulding to floating then back again; floating to flying and back again, and so forth. Investigate.

You may be beginning to imagine how this technique could be used in a performance. You may also find your way into text to accompany this process.

Now, put the metronome onto a quick tempo. Just listen to the tempo at first. Stay with it; let it in.

When you sense it as an inner tempo, begin to bring the body fully into moulding.

Very slowly, feeling the quickness of the metronome's tempo, allow the two opposing elements – the quick tempo and the slow moulding – to give rise to a quality and sensation of fear.

Begin to bring your movement into walking, sitting and rising.

As you move about the room, engaging in any number of outward activities, occasionally stop to reconnect with the tempo, with the moulding and with the quality of fear. Ultimately, allow these elements to integrate into a 'harmonious, all-embracing whole' while speaking your text: more to yourself than to another.

Now, set the metronome to a slow tempo.

Bring your movement now to stillness. Let the altered tempo overcome the fast tempo. Take your time; it isn't a sudden change.

As you let this tempo in, begin to transform the moulding slowly into floating, as if in anticipation of some danger.

Look slowly behind you, then slowly to the right and slowly to the left. Begin to move following the metronome's slow tempo, across the room, acutely aware of your back-space.

Now come quickly into flying, letting the physical form free itself of any of the body's resistance. The flying movements are connected still with the quality and sensation of fear, against the slow metronome tick.

Slow the outward movement, taking the flying inwardly against the slow outer tempo. If you have the impulse to speak, you may wish to follow it, or simply remain silent.

Bring your movement to stillness.

Let the body, through its stillness and the slow tempo of the metronome, fill your form with a full sensation of quiet serenity while performing any physical task of your choice. Moving a chair, putting on an article of clothing, etc.

Now walk out of your inwardness and just let go of the work.

Sensation with tempo

Find a place in the room where you have some space.

We will be working with our closed eyes.[4] Shut your eyes and sense that you are surrounded by a great deal of space, which expands your movement outward. It is sheer movement, slowly or quickly. It is movement for itself – not gesture, not intention, just the sensation of your movement.

We tend to overuse the arms in movement exercises. Instead, bring the torso into movement, sensing its connection with the shoulders and arms. The back of the legs, the soles of the feet as they leave and reconnect with the floor are all part of this movement – a part of the whole. The movement is full-bodied: one unit of energy.

Open your eyes and begin to move as if you are in the *moonlight* – a sensation will follow. Don't let the sensation and the pleasure of it bring you to non-movement. The movement holds the life.

Now the movement can begin to become more subtle, quieter, slower. Take your time. Work at your own pace.

---

[4] Ted's work with closed eyes is indebted to Joanna Merlin, who worked with Chekhov in California. He believes closed eyes was her own invention.

Always work with ease: the inner sensation in the arms through the movement of the arms; the spine through the torso's movement. Move with a quality, and it gives rise to sensation.

Now let's begin to move from the quality of moonlight into the *quality of darkness*, as if moonlight slowly metamorphoses into darkness. This has a different energy. Find that energy through the body's movement itself.

The movement can be subtle.

Stay with your own pace, your own process. The primary activity we are engaged in is investigation and discovery.

Working with your eyes open, move now with the *quality of serenity*.

Find sensation through the movement of your legs, as you walk, and in your arms and torso, as you lift an object or sit and rise from a chair. You might try moving slightly backward, or slightly forward, leaning into the forward space, putting on a jacket or a scarf, or arranging your hair.

Now, add the metronome, with a *quick tempo*.

Your movement can be slow against this tempo, or it might align. This can be subtle.

How does the outer tempo affect or alter your inner reality of serenity? Does it shatter it? Does it deepen your need for serenity? Or does it simply pass over the top of your head?

Let the two contrasting realities of outer tempo and inner serenity inform and influence you. Don't manufacture a response – listen; allow it to lead you. You may be surprised by where it leads you; that's the richness of the work.

Stop the metronome, but keep the tempo there in the silence; let your being absorb it. It has something to do with you and your inner life.

Start the metronome again, this time at a *slower tempo*.

Now, take that inner life you have built, with the quality and sensation of serenity with various tempos, and move it into the space around you as a *personal atmosphere* – something you carry through the room. Do this at your own pace. It's terribly important that you stay with your own process. This is an investigation; we are always seeking.

Stay now with that personal atmosphere until it becomes a substantial reality in the space that surrounds you.

When you have arrived at a place with a strong presence, bring that into *a gesture of reaching out*. Find a point of contact. It can be an empty chair, some object in the room, or perhaps another person.

The gesture of reaching out comes out of serenity, tempo and personal atmosphere. All culminate in gesture, a gesture that reaches out of you to your point of contact.

Quality and sensation

Move quickly, with ease.

Slump over and then straighten the spine quickly.

Make a fist quickly.

Point to a fellow actor quickly.

Repeat, and give yourself over to committing to the movement and the quality, listening to how the body and soul respond.

Listen to the inner echo of the outer movement. *We are seeking to discover how outer movement influences the inner life.*

Freely explore walking, sitting, picking up an object, greeting a fellow actor, doing all quickly.

Allow yourself to be awake to images, imaginations, sensations that may arise.

Stay with the activity. Be alert to what stirs in you, how your inner life responds.

Penetrate your movements with *ease*; feel as if you have stepped into a pool of ease. Resist trying too hard, as that can create tension and diminish other possible responses.

What is it to be in your body when you are moving quickly?

Stop now and then and listen to what is resonating within.

Moving in what would be a normal pace for you, see if you can maintain the sensation of moving quickly. Be awake to whatever your response is.

Do not rush this process; give yourself permission to stay with it, to find out what you can discover from moving with a specific quality.

Now change and begin to move *slowly*, not quickly. This is a significant change.

Notice how the atmosphere in the room changes. Every movement you make is slow.

Return to the spine, lengthening it slowly, making a fist slowly, pointing slowly.

Listen to how the body resonates to moving slowly. Let the quality do the work for you.

Be aware of the change that may have taken place in your feeling/sensing/imaginative life when you changed from quick to slow.

Stay with moving slowly. Commit to the activity itself, and be available to what it may awaken. Take your time.

How you move carries content; has its own life. Be awake to what arises within you.

Alternate between moving slowly and quickly, staying awake to what is happening in your inner life.

Begin moving towards or moving away from your fellow actor.

Take the quality you choose to move in from the contact you make with the other actor: a quick or slow movement towards or away from the other.

The focus is on how you move and the subsequent sensation: the feeling life that originates from that movement.

We seek to evoke a sensation: an experience felt bodily that arises from how you move. You move with a quality that, in turn, produces a sensation.

Reflect on what you have done. Let it go; file it away in your inner being.

Chekhov suggests raising and lowering an arm with caution.[5] Try this now.

Engage with a single focus in the movement and listen for any slight inner response or sensation.

Move one arm, and then the other, *cautiously*.

Begin to walk, allowing the feet to touch the floor cautiously. You are finding out something about caution through your movement. Inner/outer movement is the theme here.

Continue to make your way through the room. Sit, stand, greet another. Surrender to being actively engaged, seeking

---

[5] *To the Actor*, 58–9.

always to be awake to what your movement has to reveal to you about the quality of caution. The body may tell you something that you do not know about caution. The body knows more than you do.

Be content with seeking: free of asking too much, free of demand. Trust in the body's wisdom. Stay focused on what the body is doing. If you are stuck in a tempo, change it. It may reveal something more to you. The caution lives in the hands, in the feet, in the legs, in the back.

What is the sensation that comes to meet you through the movement?

Resist the temptation to know what caution is and perform it. It would then remain an idea in the head and lead to indicating. We seek to bypass the head and arrive at a sensation: an inner feeling response through movement, not thinking.

While moving cautiously, stop now and then and listen to what it is to be you at this moment; to what is resonating within.

Be patient. Take time. Stay open to not knowing what your response will be. Stay with the movement.

Contact your fellow actor while continuing to have a single focus, moving cautiously. How do you approach another? Do you choose to reach out? Perhaps you decide to keep your distance.

Does a tempo suggest itself? Perhaps it does, perhaps not. Listen for it. Engage it freely.

What about a direction? Is there a particular direction you are attracted to – do you have more of a desire to move into the front-space or back-space?

Stop now and then and be attuned to where you experience caution in the body.

Do not feel rushed to accomplish a full-bodied sensation. Stay with being actively engaged in movement. Listen to what you are experiencing at the moment. Live into what has been awakened.

Then breathe out. Release, let it go.

The process remains the same with all of the qualities you investigate. Engage in full-bodied movement. Exploring through movement is the key.

There are many qualities to explore. Try, for example, playfully and tenderly. You can also build upon a series of qualities. Continue to upgrade; try quietly-gently-serenely, slowly-confidently-courageously or quickly-urgently.

Quality and sensation through straight line and curved line

Bring the body into an exploration of a *straight line*, finding it in the spine's uprightness, sensing that it runs through the entire body as a purely outward physical experience and sensation.

Investigate this further with the arms out straight, making straight lines with the arms in the air, in the open space around you.

Break the arm at the elbow and sense the two straight lines created by the right angle of the bent elbow.

Try a straight leg, then a leg bent at the knee, creating two straight lines.

Sense the reality of a physical body made up of straight lines, and in your investigation of this, begin to take it in more and more as an inner experience.

Slowly begin to let go of the physical body until it becomes an inner experience as it reaches the character boundary.

As you move about the room, feel questions arise: who is this person? Do I know them? Are they perhaps very efficient, essential, organized and dependable? Or maybe someone not so pleasant? Let these questions arise independently of your own will: out of the work and investigation of a straight line.

Stay in that place of arrival, bringing in text somewhere along the way.

Now, bring the body to stillness and allow the work to release. Just move about the room in a free and open state. Release and let the body remember what you've done, noting what condition your body is in.

Now slowly begin creating *curved lines* with your arms, your hands, your spine. As you bend the elbows and the wrists, experience them inwardly as a curve. Without having to bend too far forward, sense the back, the spine, as a curved line. Find the curve by rounding the shoulders forward one at a time, so that you begin creating for yourself an experience of the body as a series of curves.

This imaginary physical reality corresponds with an inner reality. Perhaps you even have an emotional response.

Working with what you've found, you can begin to experience character – who is this person?

The roundness of the curve is another world altogether from a straight line. What does this world of curves give rise to, in all its aspects? What intention? What tempo? What temperament?

Let it take you where it will, physically as well as inwardly. This is an important aspect of the work – how it plays on your inner life.

Is this person tall? Are they short? Let the answer come out of your investigation, allowing the resolution to take you into text.

Now let's quickly bring the body into a *straight line*. Just go easy. Using your arms, legs, torso, spine, revisit that straight-line reality. What is it?

Allow it eventually to become a purely inner experience, an inner reality. That's what we are after.

Leaving you alone in your investigation, I will at some point clap my hands to signal the beginning of a change. Then you will slowly begin the process of metamorphosing: of changing that straight-line experience into a *curved-line* reality. (Clap)

Take your time; it's not to be rushed.

You have grown out of a straight line into a curve: a totally different inner reality. Don't feel a need to express or show it. The process itself, if it is authentic, will communicate the event.

Thinking about straight lines and curves is potent; it provides a valuable process to engage for moments of significant change. These changes can be used during the process of a scene or over the arc of the play, from the beginning of the play to its end.

Personal atmosphere

Find your way into the upright. Feel the verticality. Drop over from the waist and release your weight down.

As you find yourself straightening into the upright again, sense the counter-movement of your feet digging into the earth.

Repeat this several times, sensing your movement going up and down simultaneously.

Find what it is to be in readiness for the staccato/legato exercise, followed by sending out into the six directions of space, engaging two different dynamics of movement, and returning to home base between each direction.

Sense what it is to open into the space around you, make it available to you and be at the centre of space that has been opened in six different directions.

Take an imaginary ball into the back-space, and release it into the front-space.

Discover what it is to give entirely into the front-space, and then receive fully into the back-space, actively engaging with the space.

Find a partner and continue finding the possibility of opening to the space behind when receiving and into the front when giving, as you continue throwing an imaginary ball.

Awaken the belly, the head, the chest into full-bodied movement, consciously.

What is it to be curious about your every movement? What is it to be curious about your spatial relationship to another, about how much space there is between you?

What happens to you if you are close to another, too close, far away or too far away?

Return to yourself, and sense your own personal space. Seek to create a bubble of space around you, which you are at the centre of.

There is space around you, above and below you, to the right and left of you and to the front and back. Sense that you occupy this space, it belongs to you. Become thoroughly familiar and intimate with that space.

Allow yourself to move, being at the centre of your space.

Invite an image into that bubble of space: *a warm blanket around you*. Find how you can be available and genuinely open to receiving this image; be present to it. Begin to consciously engage with it, allowing it to influence you. Take your time.

Luxuriate in the possibility that it offers, actively seeking a connection. See how receptive you can be to allowing it to affect you. Is there a sensory response?

How do you move when you have the warmth of that blanket around you? Know and recognize that you can't escape it, as it defines who you are. You have put it on like a garment, and it surrounds you.

Find inner space for the effect of that imagination. Appeal to the artist within you as you seek an honest artistic response. The body remains at ease and is listening.

You have received an image into your bubble of space. What does it stir in you?

What direction do you want to move in?

Do you wish to move in straight or curved lines?

How do you hold your hands?

What is your occupation?

Are you married?

Do you live in the country or the city? A house or an apartment?

What is your name?

Is there a quality of movement that suggests itself? Continue opening, discovering who this person is.

How are you dressed? What's on your feet?

Seek to stay connected to the imagination and the life it chooses to offer.

Don't feel obligated to answer all of these questions. Listen to the ones that are provocative and interest you.

This is not a checklist; it is an artistic process, an exploration, an engagement which you are invited to follow.

Go to a classmate and speak: 'Yes', 'No' or 'Maybe'.

What is it to contact another?

Seek to surrender to the activity provoked by this image. Listen to what it reveals when you are in relation to another.

See if you can remain open to the image continuing to evolve.

If you've settled into one tempo, try changing it. Remember, a warm blanket is guiding and informing you.

Occasionally stop and listen to yourself.

Who is this? Who have you brought to life?

How is your body responding? Does it choose to soften? Are you at ease?

Look out and discover your perspective, your perception of the world, as influenced by being enveloped in a warm blanket.

Is there a particular sensation that has arisen?

How is your inner life responding?

After taking the time you need to be acutely aware of your experience, you may walk out of it, let it go, release it and allow it to trail away behind you.

Before going to another imagination, allow time to locate the space around you: the bubble of space that you are at the centre of.

Return to the same atmosphere several times, approaching it anew each time, being interested in how it evolves and continues to reveal itself.

You might like to explore some other atmospheres: *a gentle rain, a dark cloud, deep purple, a block of ice, a swarm of insects, birdsong, golden light, bubbling champagne*. Allow sufficient time for each atmosphere to reveal itself, to make itself known.

While exploring each atmosphere, you can engage the following questions:

- What do your hands want to do?
- What do your feet want to do?
- How do you want to move, and at what tempo?
- How do your arms want to move?
- How does it affect your breathing?
- If you touch something, how do you do that?
- Does a gesture or an objective suggest itself?
- How do you sit?
- How do you view the world?
- Can you give a sound to it?
- Where in the body do you experience its influence the most?
- How would you describe the inner sensation of this atmosphere?
- How can you allow the personal atmosphere to play you?
- Is the quality that suggests itself one of earth, water, air or fire?
- What direction of space presents itself?

This may require a kind of surrender on your part. What does it mean to surrender to an image, or to allow yourself to be played? Perhaps you are met with a sense of wonder that is awakened through engaging fully with an imagination.

Ensemble and objective atmosphere

Surround yourselves with the particular light that's in the room right now. Let's say it's dim. Allow yourself to be encompassed by this dimness: the space behind you, before you, above you. This dimness brushes the face, the back of the neck. It rests on the top of the head. We move through it, this semi-darkness.

As we become conscious of the presence of the light in the room, we can allow it to affect us – to alter us somehow. It surrounds us, touches us.

Move an arm through it slowly, as if it is smoke or mist.

You might experience a change of mood; for example, if the room is dim, a certain dimness of your inner light. Be content to stay with this exploration for a time.

Now let's add something to this sense, allowing it to give rise to *a sense of danger*. Resist acting fear. Join the danger to the quality of the light, without forcing yourself to feel danger.

Let it come from outside: from the atmosphere, not the intellect.

Open yourself to this atmosphere of danger.

Now, not disregarding the present atmosphere you have created as an ensemble, find a place to sit with your eyes closed.

Imagine a small stone village which has been destroyed by war. It may be high on a hill or in a valley. Be specific as you imagine its size, the colour of the stone, the individual buildings and houses destroyed, the rubble. When you feel you have a clear picture, open your eyes and put those images into the space we're in. Walk into those images – through the old, stone, war-torn village.

Be clear about what you are stepping over, what you are seeing. You're surrounded by ruins.

Sense once again this atmosphere of danger.

Your ensemble members are doing the same. You are putting the atmosphere out into the space, as they are doing; it abides outside of yourself.

You move through it. It is in the air around you. Again, resist any impulse to act fear. Let it come to you, surround you.

Simply try to be in harmony with this imaginary atmosphere. It will move you; it will speak to you: 'You are in danger'.

What is your relationship to this village? Was it your home? Or are you in foreign terrain, enemy territory? Let these questions arise out of atmosphere and place. Those aspects will lead you.

You are surrounded by danger. Let images arise out of that atmosphere. Radiate those images outward to the ensemble; don't keep them to yourself.

You are building something together, each of you, making and experiencing what you create.

Now the danger is moving closer. Sense it; feel its proximity. You must find a place of safety in the ruins.

Where are you now? A ruined house? Near a high wall? In plant growth of some kind? What objects surround you? Are there natural elements? Household items left behind? Be specific. Create a reality for yourselves. It is a constant process.

If this was your village, you know what it was before its destruction. The place you're hiding in was a place familiar to you.

If this is foreign terrain, you are totally lost in the rubble.

Your activity is one of seeking. Working with a certain place, certain circumstances, led, inspired and directed by the atmosphere.

Imaginary body

Let's begin with an exploration of the sense of form before examining an imaginary body.

The imaginary body seeks to alter the way we perceive and experience our own form.

Spend some time looking out the window at the architecture of the buildings, being acutely aware of the forms you see.

Notice how a form changes when it is juxtaposed against another form.

Find a tree and focus on its form.

Come into the space we're working in, and be awake to the form of this space, not just looking but really seeing, being specific in what you see.

Continue to be acutely aware of the forms in the space. What does this ask of you, this particular focus of attention?

As a group, begin sensing the form you are creating in the space through your spatial relationship to one another.

Change that relationship and seek to put an equal amount of space between you, filling the space with your individual forms and the form you create as an ensemble.

Shift your attention to your own physical form. How long is your neck? How broad are your shoulders? How large are your hands? How long are your legs? How round is your head? Be as specific as you can, finding a feeling/sensing relationship to your own form.

Now begin to alter your perception by inviting an image of *your legs being made of spun glass*. Give your attention entirely to engaging in this imagination. Put it on like a garment and find what comes to meet you. It may mean you have to relinquish control and give yourself over to it. Be patient, and resist manipulating the body in any way.

Explore allowing the image to dictate how you move. How does it invite you to walk, run, sit, pick up an object, relate to others?

It may suggest a particular direction. What is your experience of the front-space, the back-space?

Is a tempo suggested? Quickly? Slowly? Is it staccato? Legato?

Trust that the imagination will guide you, lead you and inform you. Attempt, through the imagination, to incorporate a body that's not your own.

How open and receptive can you be to allowing this imagination to influence you?

Add to this image that *you have tiny feet*. Try to penetrate that part of the body consciously.

Give yourself permission to not know where this image will take you, physically and emotionally. Appeal to the imagination to find an experience of a body unlike your own. Focus your concentration on the image, acknowledging that there is no way you can dictate to yourself what the influence of these images will be. Let the image guide and inform you.

Keep your focus on the image, constantly extending an invitation to live with this image as your present reality. Trust the power of the imagination.

Play with tempo and direction, while sitting, crossing your legs, standing, picking up a chair.

Search for who this might be as you engage in these various activities. Find out what it is to live in this other body.

The body will change itself, as the physical body will gradually merge with the imaginary body.

Find a partner and exchange a line of text.

What is your response when contacting another? How is the text influenced by this particular imaginary body?

What might this person's gesture be?

Sense what is resonating in you. What has living into this imagination awakened in you? Absorb what has been given to you, the sensation that has arisen through this image. Trust your own experience, eliminating the need to feel that there is a right or wrong response.

Then, let it go, clear yourself and return to owning and experiencing your own form. Be awake to the difference when returning to what is known to you.

You now have *short, stubby legs*. They are squashed, compact. You may have an immediate response to this, or none at all. Acknowledge and accept whatever experience or sensation arises.

We seek to strengthen and trust the power of an image, of the imagination, to influence us.

Tell yourself you don't have to show anything. You can dare to be boring.

You seek to find out how an image plays into your inner life and how it affects the rest of the body.

Allow an emotional feeling or content to arise. Take the time you need.

Add to the short, stubby legs *a large rear end*. If it's too much to sense both the legs and the rear end, shift your focus from one to the other.

Nothing has to be shown or displayed outwardly. This is for you: you're exploring how it affects you; how it affects the experience of yourself, both physically and psychically.

How do you keep the images alive?

At some point, choose to exhibit the influence of this imaginary body outwardly. Does this increase your ability to respond to the image's influence? Incorporate it inwardly as your secret again.

Go to someone and have a brief conversation, with the words, 'Yes', 'No' or 'Maybe'.

Listen to how you respond when coming into contact with another and how you speak these words. How do you receive the words that are spoken to you?

Let go of the outer activity. Stand and listen to what it is to be you at this moment.

Acknowledge fully what your experience has been: the sensation you have brought to life.
Allow yourself to appreciate who or what you have brought to life, and then let it go. Walk away from it, and return to your own known body and form.

Stick, ball, veil

You have each been given an *imaginary stick*.

Investigate the qualities inherent in it thoroughly. Its length, width, texture, weight and colour.

All of your sticks are different; each is a stick you have chosen. What is common to all is the fact that it is straight.

Get to know your stick and what you can and cannot do with it. Investigate stick-ness, straightness. What is it?

Begin to invest something of yourself into how you handle your stick. Move with it, carry it, drag it, throw it into the air, befriend it. Seek to gently breathe it in, taking it within yourself, swallowing it whole. The stick is no longer separate from you, as you have attempted to become one with it.

Seek to make known within yourself all of the qualities of your stick, such as how heavy, long, narrow or wide it is. Allow the qualities of the stick to become your own. Explore and incorporate what appeals to you about stick-ness. Continue to listen as it whispers its tempo, direction, gesture and centre to you.

Who is this? What has it awakened in you? Do you recognize that in you which is stick-like?

You've been given a toy. Play.

Find pleasure in discovering how you can take on the being of a stick.

Experiment saying a line of text, speaking to another.

What's your profession? Your name? What is your perception of the world?

Allow the stick to have its own integrity and to play you.

See if you can get out of the way and become open to receiving the qualities of your stick.

Be still and listen to what you've brought to life, to acknowledge and accept what your process has been, free of demand and expectation. Is there a sensation that has arisen that could be related to the qualities of a stick? Of being straight?

Then, let it go. Shake free of the concentration. Come back fully to your experience in your body, in this space, with these actors.

Now, you have each been given *an imaginary ball*.

Each of your balls is unique. The common thread is that it is round. What is round? Investigate being round.

What is the size of your ball? Is it huge, like a beach ball, or small, like a baseball? How light is it? What colour? Does it have a life of its own?

Open yourself to receiving the nature of being round, as you're giving all of your attention to it.

It's round, not curved, not a circle. Does it bounce? Roll? Can you throw it into the air? How fast or slow does it roll? How high does it bounce?

Begin to delicately entertain the possibility that the ball is inviting you to swallow it whole, becoming one with it.

You are all round; you have no sharp edges. Find out how you make your way through the space. Do you roll along? Do you bounce?

Let the roundness of the ball reveal itself, its life, to you. Remain standing.

Get to know this roundness by relinquishing control, surrendering to being round. Nothing is being required of you except to surrender to being round.

Roundness has been given to you as an imagination to play with, to expand your capacity for transformation through swallowing whole an object: in this instance, a round ball.

Be willing to be bold and exaggerate your roundness.

Your inner being is a big, open, round space filled with air.

Follow your impulse in terms of how you walk, run, sit, speak.

Contact another. At some point, let go of how the roundness manifests outwardly, and make the fact that you are round your secret.

Occasionally stop and listen to how this exploration resonates in you – is there a sensation? It may be something you know well, or it may be foreign to you. Whatever it is, absorb the sensation, breathe it in a little deeper, before breathing it out and letting it go.

Allow yourself to let go.

Now you have been given an *imaginary veil*.

Find out for yourself what a veil is, its qualities. How light is it? What is its colour? Does it have a form that it can sustain?

Remember, this is your creation. What is it to have no weight?

If you toss it into the air, what form does it take when it lands on the floor?

Play. Get to know your veil. At some point, become one with your veil, swallow it. There is no separation between you and it.

Allow the veil to continue to reveal itself to you. The body listens to the life it gives to you. The body becomes one with it.

Feel free to move between exaggerating the veil's life and making it your secret.

Fall in love with getting to know your veil. Is your inner response something familiar to you, or is it unknown?

Explore how you sit and walk, and how your feet touch the floor. Explore direction, tempo, even name and profession.

How fully does the veil occupy the fullness of your body?

What is your favourite music? How do you dance?

Take a moment to be still and listen to what is stirring in you.

Look out into the space. Look at one another. Find out if your perception of the world around you is altered by incorporating the qualities of a veil.

Be willing to acknowledge your creation, and then walk away, releasing it into the back-space.

Archetypes

Find yourself in relation to the space you occupy.

Become acutely aware of the back-space.

Sense you are being followed. Give yourself time to live into this suggestion, to contemplate it. Imagine this somebody or something is much more powerful than you are. There is an entity accompanying you.

Become interested in this potential, this possibility. This being, this entity has a life independent of you. Be awake to its presence.

What is it to be open and available to the unknown and genuinely curious? Stay curious.

This presence is the archetype of *the orphan*.

Sense the orphan following you, wanting to be known. An orphan is accompanying your every movement. This orphan can also walk beside you and in front of you. Where does this image take you? What does it stir in you?

Allow your creative self some time to be affected; to want to become acquainted and gently wish to unite with this being.

Seek to want to experience the world from the orphan's perspective. Leave yourself open to find out what you can discover.

Ask the orphan to inform you of its wants and needs. Seek to bypass preconceived ideas and listen to what is being revealed.

Step into the world of the orphan; surrender to the reality of the orphan's life. How would you physicalize its needs, wants, desires, intentions?

Listen the orphan into being within yourself. Let yourself be played.

What are the primary qualities of the orphan? How do you give expression to being alone, abandoned, perhaps enraged?

Be patient and enjoy – appreciate – this possibility of getting to know someone previously unknown.

Give yourself permission to listen and be receptive to this existence that is within your presence, gradually invading your physical body, your feeling life.

Be willing to experiment with many gestures. Try a reach or a pull.

What does the orphan want? Engage in a quest to become intimate with the inner life of the orphan. No result is required. Stop and listen; observe yourself. What is your experience of your physical and feeling life?

Resume your listening and your quest for a *gesture*. Listen for a *direction*, for a *tempo*. Imagine the orphan whispering in your ear, guiding you in your search for a gesture.

What is the primary quality of the orphan? Is it longing? Extreme tenderness? Possibly fear or caution? Maybe desperation? Play with these and other possibilities.

Unite a *quality* with a *gesture*, *reaching longingly* or perhaps *pulling desperately*. Discover what you can as each gesture and quality presents itself. Allow yourself to explore.

Fall in love with being an investigator, putting gently aside preconceptions. Get to know the orphan as you walk together, side by side, and as you choose to become united.

This process of placing the archetype in the space around you, listening it into being, making space within to allow it to influence you, is one way into discovering archetypes, as well as the psychological gesture of the archetype.

You might find it helpful to refer back to the list of archetypes set out in Part 3.[6]

Awakening to gesture

The following exercises might be explored over several classes.

---

[6] The List of Archetypes is on page 55.

Take time to consciously inhabit the body and the space. Find out what this means to you. When working with gesture, the fullness of the body must be available and participating.

Be aware of allowing the body to wake up instead of feeling that you have to force or demand an awakening. Be accepting of what you can sense is available to you in the moment.

Exercise 1

Begin to find out what happens inwardly if you change how you throw an imaginary ball. For example, overhand, as hard as possible. What sensation does this evoke in you? What might you want to achieve?

Soften the body and send the imaginary ball flying through the air. *Throw* the imaginary ball *down forcefully*.

This is gesture and direction with a quality.

You could be destroying or crushing something.

While continuing to throw the imaginary ball, begin to explore changing *direction* and *tempo*, opting to add staccato and legato.

See if the body can remain loose, and take time to listen to the body and how it responds with each throw.

You are not asking anything of the throw other than *how* you throw it, the *direction* of the throw and *how* it plays back on you.

Since we are in the area of gesture, is this a gesture if you open your arms fully into the horizontal from the imaginary centre?

Is it a gesture that carries the intention to open?

Does another gesture suggest itself?

What makes it a gesture?

In further entering into the life and world of gesture, seek to give to the space.

Slice through the space. *Tear* the space. The space is your partner, the one you're engaging and playing with. *Caress. Punch. Embrace.*

These gestures engage the body giving expression, recognizing what it already knows about gesture.

Exercise 2

Kick the space. Continue to engage in kicking; do it *playfully*.

Begin to engage with the other actors in the room with your playful kick. Take great care not to touch them, but have the kick and intention in the space between you.

Carry that playful kick inwardly, being awake to the possibility that a kick could burst forth from you at any moment.

Remember, it is playful.

You carry an inner gesture of kick. It's your secret, and you are awake to the possibility that the kick will want to be expressed at any moment. That playful kick fills you.

It is a potential that you are carrying.

Because the potential is there, it gives you life.

Exercise 3

I am going to give a series of common expressions. Allow yourself to be open to receiving the expression's thoughts, and respond with a physical gesture.

The task is not to think about it but to allow yourself to respond intuitively, to receive the words, and let the body give expression to the thought.

Sufficient time will be given to each expression so that you can explore it fully.

The first expression is, 'Come here'.

Allow yourself to let the face go and give fully to finding the expression with the whole body.

Whisper the words of the expression, joining them with the outer activity of the gesture.

Listen to how that expression resonates in you.

Seek the many different dynamics the phrase can have – a command, a pleading, a teasing, a coaxing and so on.

The body will interpret what this means to you, whether you direct it to a child, a lover or someone who needs help.

Listen to what you are doing, as an intention may arise: to seduce, to give comfort, to tease and to dominate. Now let's try some others:

'No, don't'.

'How dare you'.

'It wasn't me'.

How does the body choose to express each of these thoughts? What happens to you inwardly, to your sensing/feeling life as you express them?

How do you join the inner soul experience with the outer gesture, becoming one with the gesture, the inner and the outer joining in one full-bodied gesture?

Let the fullness of the body speak.

Each of these expressions could embody many different intentions.

We are playing with the fact that something spontaneously arises in the form of movement when we hear a particular known phrase.

Chekhov suggests we are always in gesture, so I ask you, what gesture am I, the teacher, in right now?[7]

Let's try some more:

'I want to grasp the idea.'

'I want to give comfort.'

'I want to hide.'

'I want to protect myself.'

'I want to dominate the room.'

Walk, carrying the inner reality of the expression and the gesture as potential. Develop the sense that your inner life is filled with that expression.
The next step is to hear the expression, take it in, but hold off giving expression outwardly. Let it live in you; let it fill you with its content.

'I want someone to help me.'

Stay with it, continuing to take the content in, allowing it to resonate in you.

When you feel you have to release it into space, when something needs to burst forth, do you give it outer expression in the form of a gesture?

When you have found how to feed it into a gesture, listen to what you have done, and repeat.

Repeat the gesture that expresses your need several times; listen to how it resonates with you. Seek to carry it inwardly.

Go to someone and say, 'I want someone to help me'.

---

[7] Fern's answer to this in the class was 'I sense myself reaching, and you are leaning in, opening to receive. I'm going out, but I am taking you in simultaneously.'

Exercise 4

This is another exploration.

Find a partner. One of you wants to hug the other, and the other does not want to be embraced.

Take time to live into this scenario.

If you do not want to be hugged, perhaps you want to keep your partner at a distance, to get them to stay away, so they can't touch you.

What gestures arise through this particular desire?

Psychological gesture – adding quality and objective

Find your way into executing the archetypal, full-bodied gesture of *reach*. Repeat it several times to get it into the body and space.

Try *reaching tenderly* when you feel you have established a relationship with reach.

Stay with it. Repeat reaching tenderly.

Does a want or need suggest itself?

Continue to sense what is aroused within as a possible desire. It could be to give comfort, to offer help, to protect or to want recognition.

Reach tenderly and listen.

Again.

What stirs in your feeling life? Acknowledge and accept whatever presents itself. Doing all with ease is essential.

Now *reach playfully*.

What happened to the tempo? What stirred in your feeling life? How is this experience different from reaching tenderly? What could your need be?

We now have the *gesture* with *quality*, the *what* and the *how*. *Why* are you reaching tenderly or playfully?

The objective, need, want, desire and intention are *why*.

If you *reach longingly*, a different need will arise. Perhaps you need help for yourself. If you *reach desperately*, maybe the need is to rescue another. If you *reach cautiously*, perhaps you are seeking contact.

Try these qualities one at a time, giving some time to each, and find for yourself what need arises.

Listen to your response; the movement and the quality will awaken a response to the reality of an objective.

Listen for it.

Resurrect the gesture of *pull* in your body and space. Begin to *pull tenderly*.

Why are you doing this? What is it you want? Are you needing sympathy, or perhaps companionship? Are you wishing to close the distance between you and the other?

What arises within you?

Try *pulling playfully*, perhaps to tease.

Pull confidently, to wake another up.

Pull sadly, in need of sympathy.

Pull cautiously, to reassure.

Continue to seek to embody the gesture and the quality, allowing the activity to reveal to you the objective.

The *gesture* and *how* you execute it enable the fulfilment or realization of the *objective*. Thus, we have the psychological gesture: the *what, how* and *why*.

You can ask which comes first: the gesture, the desire, the how?

Just enjoy the seeking!

Listen to the imagination, movement, impulse, and follow them; see where they take you.

Using a mask to explore archetypal gestures

Simply take us in. You are wearing your neutral mask. You are being witnessed. You are being seen. Take that in. Sense us.
Sense the neutral mask and what it may do to you. Make it all conscious.

Now begin to find that archetypal gesture of *push*; find it physically. Let the fullness of the body once again discover and express push. Remember, the push goes somewhere, from you out to us.

Put the arms down after a few attempts; you are just testing it.

You may now have a different relationship with the body due to the mask.

It's important that you let all changes that you might be experiencing be conscious. Be with yourself in a superconscious way. Conscious, wakeful availability is what the mask can do for you; that's our purpose in working with it.

The hands have to be conscious and active. The push is in the palms of the hands.

Keep looking for the gesture physically. Let your body listen to the push forward.

When you feel you have embodied it, take off the mask, allowing the gesture to have a life in you, and turn to us without the mask, still connected with the inner gesture.

Take us in. Sense the space between.

Put that gesture as an inner gesture gently into the room, into the space – *playfully, or aggressively, or cautiously*: however you wish. Speak the text from the inner gesture, the inner motion.

Play with the space between, keeping in mind that the gesture is in that space between – that's where the drama is, in the space between.

Choices, contact and point of focus

This was a class given to actors experiencing a lack of confidence in making and executing choices on stage. The intention was to try to bring clarity: to see making a choice as a simple act, deciding on a point of focus. This exercise is worth spending some time on: thoroughly explore and investigate the ideas it presents.

Let's walk freely, with no particular intention or purpose. We can stop now and again, find ourselves and ask, 'What's my inner tempo today?'

When I clap, I want you to contact your arms; connect to the way that you are swinging your arms.

Simply that. You can change it, or stop it, or just notice it. (Clap)

Just focus on what appears to be the natural swing and movement of the arms as you walk.

Now stop all movement.

Contact your feet.

Move them, quickly or slowly, and notice their contact with the carpet. If you are wearing shoes, remove them to make the connection more sensory. Notice the softness of the carpet or the hardness of the concrete.

Imagine walking on the warm sand at the beach, or in mud.

Both give you an acute awareness of the soles of the feet.

Now contact the space behind you. If you are moving forward, it moves with you. If you contact an object in that space behind you, the distance increases as you move forward.

Move backward toward it.

If this concentration causes any physical tension, focus on that tension and allow it to release.

Now change your attention to the hands.

Without looking at them, inwardly contact them. Feel their shape and form, and sense the space between the fingers. Your ability to contact can be that specific.

Now contact a place inside, in your lower belly. Just rest inwardly there, in the warmth of that lower physical location.

Carry it with you as you walk freely around the room.

You are sitting or rising or putting on an article of clothing, or simply staying with that physical centre's sensation.

Now let's be a little creative with that physical centre. Uniting your imagination with that physical place, give it a soft, warm-dough quality. It works back on you, this creative activity, which is psycho-physical.

It takes you now away from yourself, going towards character.

After some time, you can change the quality of this centre you've created, through simple contact, into a hard, cold stone sitting in the belly.

You may find yourself changed as it works back on you. Walk with that centre in your belly. Don't lead it; it leads you.

Now stop all movement, drop your focus and walk out of it. Let yourselves be free.

Stretch, breathe deeply, lie on the floor and release all unwanted tension down into the floor. Just lie there like a wet noodle, a strand of spaghetti.

When you feel able to do so, rise from the floor and contact that lower centre again; reconnect to it. It's there, available for you and for your attention.

It's just a matter of a point of focus.

An exercise for the last week of class: an invitation

In the last week of class, Fern and Ted put a list of character descriptions alongside a list of tools up on a whiteboard.

They use this list to fire up the actors' memory and imagination, and guide their choices. It's a bridge for actors to begin claiming the technique as their own.

The character descriptions given here resemble something you might receive prior to an audition: they are general and limited. The question we are seeking to answer here is: how does one create a character with the Chekhov tools with broad, limited information *and* with limited time?

Here are the lists.

Tools	Character descriptions
Intention	
Psychological gesture	1 Male, blue-collar worker: • manly, not intellectual, a good mate; *or* • slow, manly, kind.
Archetypes	
Personal atmosphere	2 Female, career woman: • clear, sharp in her criticism, cutting in her humour; *or* • efficient, bright, clear.
Expanding/ contracting	
Qualities/ sensations	3 Any gender, large, clumsy, stupid, understands nothing: • grumpy, perhaps even cruel; *or* • kind.
Tempo	
	4 Male, gentle, refined, every movement is ballet-like, graceful yet manly: • kind, open, *or* • a total snob.
	5 Female, willowy, graceful, feminine: • kind, open, *or* • a total snob.
	6 Any gender, short, thick legs, big head, stiff joints, bulldog: • open, good-natured; *or* • scowling, silent, taciturn.

Ted and Fern encourage the actors to play with all the tools on the board and settle on one or two choices: those that resonate or feel the most potent.

On the last day, Fern and Ted ask actors to write down all the tools the class have learnt on the whiteboard and repeat the character description exercise.

This time, the actors have many choices to consider. They are guided to play with all the tools and then to settle on one or two, maybe three, if they could manage them. Ted and Fern stress that it's important not to load up on too many. They encourage actors to really explore a chosen tool in detail.

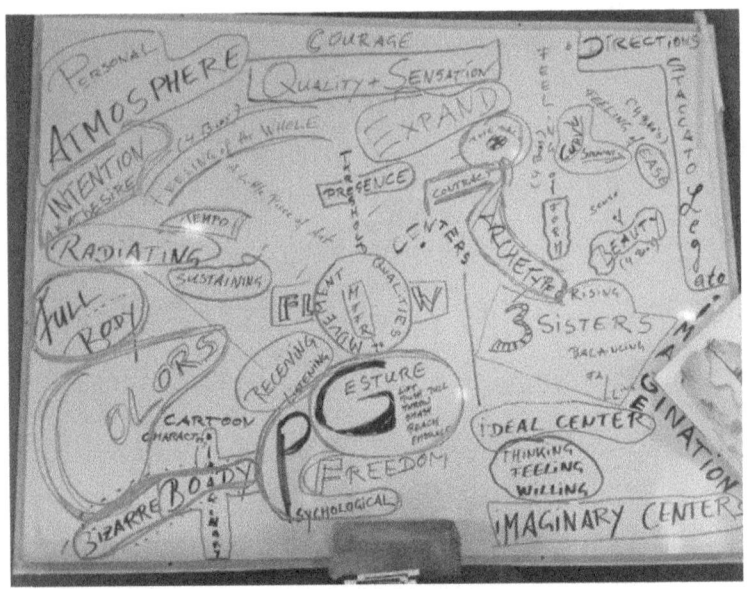

FIGURE 7 *The Distance Travelled, 2015. Photography by Danielle Carter*

FIGURE 8 *Fern Sloan, 2015. Photography by Peggy Coffey*

Part 6

Some guidance for teaching the Chekhov work

Fern and Ted are aware that there are those who may feel, like they both did, a calling not just to practise this work but to teach it. This part presents some brief guidance for those who may experience this calling.

When Ted and Fern began teaching this work, it was in response to an intense desire on their parts to find a way to make this treasure trove available to others. The two note that teaching has also given them an incredible gift for their own sakes: the opportunity to keep engaging in what the Chekhov work offers in a very human sense: investigating, researching and discovering the limitless capacities within the human organism, the wonder of the physical form and the wisdom of the body. Uncovering the inexhaustible levels of meaning revealed through this work is a constant source of new life for Ted and Fern, a treasure. It is something to wrestle with eagerly; it brings a needy world meaning, beauty and understanding. The two note that seeking to penetrate the physical/tangible with non-tangible realities is the work of a lifetime.

A teacher of the Chekhov work may, firstly, need to resolve some common misconceptions about what the work actually entails.

Misconceptions about the Chekhov technique

Speaking of some common misconceptions, *Fern says*:

> Some believe that Chekhov's work is just a series of very simple exercises. But the technique in its essence is about getting out of the head and surrendering to the body's wisdom. This takes doing; it takes practice. Michael Chekhov gave the actor scales, just as the musician has scales. Why should the actor feel exempt from such a discipline and commitment to developing capacities?

> One of the most considerable difficulties in accessing the work is trust. It takes trust to sense that you can move in a certain way and awaken activity within, to enliven the inner life through outer movement. It takes a lot of individual seeking on the actor's part, to really find that moment when they can say, 'I'm now experiencing something that the body is telling me that I'm not telling it.' It's worth acknowledging that the psycho/physical relationship is not always readily available as an experience.

> We are guiding students as they explore what it means to be present, open and available; what it means to be at one with their inner and outer life, to trust movement, follow an imagination and surrender to an image.

Beginning a class: training actors to become receptive

Ted and Fern note that teaching the Chekhov technique is about teaching people to become receptive to their bodies. It's all about awareness – gathering information – through movement. Classes always begin with the teachers finding themselves and inviting the student actors to find themselves. The first question asked is, 'Where are you today?' The first thing Fern and Ted are doing in each class is to ask students to be aware of what is happening with their physical body.

At the beginning of a class, Fern and Ted stress that there is nothing more valuable than listening.

Ted says:

> We say, 'I want you to find out where you are. Are you tense? Are you tired? Don't resist it, just be aware of what is going on for you.' It won't happen for the student right away. You have to give them time when you begin a class; let them become aware. Something will happen. They might say, 'Oh, man, I never realised how tired I am.' Then somebody else might say, 'I need to move.' So, they move. I'm convinced that more space and time can be given to listening than we currently give.

Teaching focus and concentration

Ted and Fern note that the Chekhov work requires intense focus and concentration. This is not necessarily something you can teach.

In this context, as a teacher, you need to be very clear about what you're asking a roomful of people to do. Don't make an instruction general, and use terms everybody in the room will have a relationship to. *Specificity* is crucial. Be specific about where the focus is.

Fern and Ted share, teachers are tempted, particularly when they are beginning to teach, to entertain their students and to move quickly, so that they are not demanding that degree of concentration, attention or focus. Students will want you to go quicker, and it's your job to go slower. Go slower than your own rhythm, which may be pretty fast.

Going slower might mean having the courage to leave students on their own for a while – avoiding looking at your watch and saying, 'I want to get to something else'. If the students are doing an activity and really discovering things, as their teacher, just be quiet for a while. Let the class explore on their own. Lead them into the inquiry of the work and then leave them there for a while.

It's important, sometimes, to allow the students to flounder; to be lost. Let them say, 'I cannot possibly expand and contract for one more minute'. When Fern and Ted dare to allow the students to struggle, they teach them more than just certain elements of the method; they teach them *how* to work. Fern and Ted both note that they learnt this lesson themselves from their own teachers, Michael Howard and Uta Hagen. Learning how to work *can* be taught. And another thing that can be taught is the lesson that this work is not superficial, and it should not be approached in that way.

The teacher has a huge job in continuing to offer something that will draw the students' attention to the task at hand. The teacher seeks to find ways to help them continue their exploration. It's important to offer not necessarily encouragements but little suggestions.

Working with young actors

Can acting actually be taught? A student in one of Ted's and Fern's classes once said to them, 'You cannot do this for us. We can only do this for ourselves'. That's true. The teacher can't do it for the student. It's up to the individual actor to find their way: the teachers, at most, offer guidance on that journey.

In the classes they teach, Fern and Ted lead. They make suggestions, but they don't say, 'No, no, that's not it, you're not doing it'. This is particularly true for young students. The teacher has to point the way. You might see that, perhaps, a student is too tense in the neck and shoulders. You might say, 'What would happen if you lowered the shoulders? See if that doesn't free you up'. Or, 'Open up the hand when you are doing staccato and legato' – with an aim to help the student sense the difference.

In coming to the Chekhov work, a lot of young people have to relearn their relationship to the body. Ted and Fern tell them, over and over again, that this work is experiential. If the actor doesn't really experience it with their whole self, they will not understand the language. They will be paying heed to some idea of the technique, but that's all – and that's not the technique.

One important thing that a teacher of the Chekhov technique can do is to always be bringing it back to the statement, 'This is what you do in real life. This isn't something new; you do it all the time.' We want to make this idea conscious, so it will be there for actors when they need it.

The teacher must embody the work themselves; must honestly know it. Otherwise, you're teaching out of an idea. The guidance needs to come out of the teacher's own inner experience of the work.

Teaching non-actors

Fern and Ted note that their degree of success in teaching non-actors has in large part been contingent on their age and physical habits.

The Chekhov work requires an availability to the physical body. Ted and Fern focus, at first, on full-body work, which means work with the three centres: the head, chest and belly. The aim is to work towards an experience of greater ease. Of the four brothers, ease makes an excellent entry point, and may be the only one of the four brothers you need to focus on. Then you could bring in qualities of movement and centres.

In teaching non-actors, Fern and Ted have found that the best entry point is to guide students in participating with the fullness of the body at all times. This allows them to experience the pleasure of movement and appeals to a sense of play, free of judgement. In this context, the teacher offers an invitation to be curious.

Teaching images

One way Ted and Fern teach the incorporation of images is by asking actors who have been working for some time on a character to sit and close their eyes and let an image of the character appear. The actor accepts whatever image arrives. The teacher then gets them up on their feet and asks them to climb into that image. The actor wears the image like clothing, returning from time to time to the inner vision and letting the image inform and enrich their work.

A teacher can use guided image work to encourage students to use images in their own practice. You can have the class close their eyes and say, 'A man is walking down a city street; there are no people around; he is carrying a briefcase'. Pause, and let the class develop that image. Then say, 'He starts to walk faster and faster, until he is running very fast. He comes to the water's edge. He throws down his briefcase and takes off his jacket, and dives into the water. He swims to an island. When he reaches the island, he sees that there is one tree, and under that tree is an object. What is the object?' This is a great way for actors to learn to trust their images.

Ted says:

Years ago, when I was teaching at the Chekhov studio, I started working with fairy tales. I would read a story with the students' eyes closed and pause in certain places. Then I would put the book down, they would open their eyes and I would say, 'Did you have an image of the door?' Of course, everybody did. It was a great way to show the students how you just have to have that image when you talk about the door and it makes that moment alive.

Another exercise that I did was to get the students to sit up against the wall in a very upright position. I asked them to close their eyes and to imagine somebody: to trust an image would come of a person. It was in New York City, where students had come through the subway, through the streets, with all kinds of people.

I did this once with some students who never went very far out on a limb; they played everything very close to their chests. I got them to imagine somebody, and suddenly they were up on their feet and doing wild kinds of characters, very truthfully. I was astounded. At the end of class, I asked, 'What just happened? You were making big choices and filling them'. One actor said, 'I felt safe because it was my image'. That was a great learning experience for me.

Teaching imaginary body, imaginary centre and gesture

Fern and Ted always begin classes with a focus on awareness, regardless of what the ultimate goal of the class is. They start with exploring where the students are and what they have available to them. In life, Fern and Ted note, we are almost all pretty unconscious below the chin. We need to slow down, find ourselves both emotionally and physically, and try to embrace that, rather than resist it. In this way, we can slowly move to a greater sense of openness and ease.

Working with imaginary body, imaginary centre and gesture is a way to bridge that gap between the emotional life and the physical body. Each is about the integration of inner and outer, the emotional life and the physical body. The way Ted and Fern teach these tools is different every time; it has to do with who's in the room and their experience with the Chekhov work. Ted and Fern would never start a class with imaginary body; they really want the actors to bring their whole selves – physical, emotional and spiritual self – to this work.

These tools are accessible to different people in different ways. Some people immediately catch on, and others flounder. The teacher guides students in edging their way in.

When introducing imaginary body, keep it playful initially, so that the actors are not turning themselves inside out trying to make themselves believe that their body is one thing or another. You might say, 'What would happen if your feet were actually two feet long? Just play with that idea and see'. Uta Hagen used to use 'as ifs': 'as if your hands are enormous . . . as if you have tiny feet'.

Ultimately, you want to be specific, and you want to ground it. Teaching imaginary body can be a great part of the class, where the students really get to play. It should always be brought to the actors in a way in which they can thoroughly enjoy what they are doing.

Fern says:

I avoided teaching imaginary body for some time, until I found out that my process was different. I couldn't get the sense of a longer arm around my body, but I could get a sense that it was my arm that was longer. This goes to show that there are many individual ways of working with these tools. For me, I really need to sense my arm. If I don't have a sense of my arm, I cannot have a sense of an imaginary arm. You have to be fully present within your own being before you can go to an imaginary body.

On using balls as a teaching aid

More often than not, Fern and Ted begin class by throwing balls. The primary activity of an actor is to give and receive: to engage in contact with another. How better to activate this than by throwing a ball?

The act of throwing and catching a ball is a transaction between people: a happening, an event. The space is filled with both the outer and the inner activity. There is direction, into the front-space and into the back-space. Ask students, 'Where does the impulse for throwing arise?' 'Can you develop a sense of creating a golden thread between you and the other that comes from the chest's ideal centre?' 'What is it take in, to see another person before you release the ball?' We are always awakening a sense of movement: following a movement, being at one with movement.

In throwing and catching, a simple deed is performed and received – a real transaction has occurred. Over weeks of doing this, we build on it, by bringing to consciousness contact, awareness and sustaining. These are all essential in the work of the psycho-physical gesture.

You can spend the first weeks with a group of students exploring how to release the ball: finding how to be in and participate with the body, experience movement and gain pleasure from that.

Fern says:

We are appealing to our students' sense of play, free of judgment. We emphasise ease; letting go of undue effort; offering an invitation to be curious explore, investigate and be free of goals.

Throwing the ball, once we make it conscious, can lead to almost any aspect of the Chekhov work.

Wrapping up

As this book has hopefully shown, the Chekhov work takes time and dedication. It's a training, like any technique. Students of this work need to dedicate themselves to repetition of the exercises, and respect for the profundity of the work itself. These techniques are not a quick fix – otherwise, Ted and Fern would not still be making discoveries after over forty years of exploring and experimenting.

One of the first plays The Actors' Ensemble did was *Nobodaddy* by Archibald MacLeish. Fern remembers going into rehearsals for the play. She hadn't done any analysis; she just started working, moving through the body, drawing on different aspects of the Chekhov work. At that point, she says, this way of working was a totally different world for her. It was movement; it was consciousness. In working in this way, she invited consciousness into her attempt to fulfil and embody the work. It was deeply satisfying to her. It opened up new worlds. Fern always returns to the wholeness – the health-giving aspect – of the Chekhov work. She stresses that there is a living aspect to this work which means you are always in process. You are always seeking, always investigating and always exploring: in a classroom, in a rehearsal room or up on the stage.

For Ted's part, he is convinced that the greatest gift the Michael Chekhov work gives an actor is the experience of becoming whole and conscious – of how you can live rightly and creatively in this physical envelope he calls our instrument. It's a consciousness of how in control you are of your human processes. Ted believes that becoming conscious of radiating, receiving, expanding, contracting and inner gesture ripens us as human beings.

After a class with Fern and Ted, actors often leave feeling they've rediscovered themselves. As they describe it, they find themselves revived and enlivened by the work. The way Ted sees it, these actors have connected to a life force.

Both Ted and Fern see this work as limitless. There is no coming to the limit of what can be revealed. Both in their eighties, the two are still on a path of discovery. They believe that the work Michael Chekhov has left us is an amazing gift.

For my own part, I've come to understand that the Chekhov work makes it possible to truly experience the body–mind connection and to allow the imagination to alter the physical, emotional and spiritual . When we trust the body – our own movement – to take us where we want to go inwardly, there's a surprising freedom that makes itself known. Michael Chekhov has given us tools to access different aspects of our being, enabling us to uncover them, digging ever deeper, constantly expanding with more and more possibilities. These exercises that we have looked at in this book allow us to build capacities that would otherwise remain unknown to us, and thus unavailable.

In undertaking the Chekhov work, we're seeking to enlarge and make conscious our sense and experience of what it is to be a human being, to inhabit the physical body and to access more of what is humanly possible.

In conclusion

I wrote this book because it was the book on the Chekhov work I longed to read. Writing it has been the gift and challenge of a lifetime.

Capturing Fern and Ted on the page through an active engagement with their practice has been a long journey; not always an easy one. However, no acting class I took before or have taken since has given me the joy, majesty, inspiration, creativity, passion and humanity that I found on the floor with Fern and Ted in Hudson. Their classes returned to me my pure joy of acting – creating – giving me the new toolbox I craved. I hope I have captured a slice of that experience in these pages.

Ted's and Fern's work continues to enrich and resonate actors' lives. Their influence remains constant. They have made Michael Chekhov's work come alive.

ACKNOWLEDGEMENTS

I can't begin without saying thank you to the original hunter of awe and creativity, Michael Chekhov – what a playground you have left us.

To Ted Pugh and Fern Sloan for the hours of work and conversations and for holding a space for us all to thrive and create in – thank you for your insatiable curiosity and trust. To the maestro of deep play, Ragnar Freidank, for believing this could be done at the beginning, for his endless hours of technical wizardry and for teaching me the art of letting go, in life and in art. Ted, Fern and Ragnar, you have given me the keys to the kingdom and shown me how to carve in snow.

To Joanna Merlin for her never-ending grace and wisdom, and for being the best cheerleader anyone could ever ask for. We miss you.

To Bethany Caputo for her no-nonsense advice, for her big heart and for her words, which float up off the page and into the body.

To Jessica Cerullo, Connie Vitale and Ulli Birvé for their direction when I was rudderless.

To Val Kissel for the beautiful drawings, and to Eddie Marritz and Jessica Maynard for the stunning photos.

To Kim Barrett Lane for her kindness and generosity, without which this book may not have existed, and to Pierre du Prey for his kind permission.

To Gabriella Bonomo, Lauren Clair, Peggy Coffey and Mark Kilmurry for their time, insights and care in reading the early drafts of the book, letting me know what was clear and what wasn't, and helping the book find its voice.

To Lisa Mann, Belinda Maxwell, Andrew Crowley, India Lopez and Daisy Coles for the support, work and sage advice.

To Anna Brewer for her support and guidance and for helping me write the book I imagined. To Sam Nicholls and Aanchal Vij for answering all the endless questions I put to them with grace and good humour.

To Louise Siversen for her guidance, support and for being of the top-shelf variety, and to Charlotte Kennedy for thinking every idea I have is a good one. To Darrell Martin for his love, patience, humour and ease, not just over the last nine years as I've been writing this but for the past twenty-five years. And, of course, as always, to Vicki.

FIGURE 9 *Fern Sloan, 2015. Photography by Edward Marritz*

FIGURE 10 *Fern Sloan, 2021. Photography by Ragnar Freidank*

FIGURE 11 *Ragnar Freidank, 2015. Photography by Eddie Marritz*

FIGURE 12 *Ted Pugh, 2018. Photography Jessica Maynard*

FIGURE 13 *Ted Pugh, 2018. Photography Jessica Maynard*

REFERENCES

Bonham-Carter, Victor. *Dartington Hall: The Formative Years*: 1925–1957. Dulverton, Somerset: The Exmoor Press, 1970.

Caracciolo, Diane. *Autobiography of Deirdre Hurst Du Prey*. Sessions 1 and 2, MC/S4/36/H, 1998.

Caracciolo, Diane. 'Deidre Hurst Du Prey: A Life Devoted to the Creative Imagination'. In *The Swing of the Pendulum: The Urgency of Arts Education for Healing, Learning and Wholeness*, edited by Diane Caracciolo and Courtney Lee Weider, 135–47. Rotterdam: SensePublishers, 2017.

Caracciolo, Diane. 'Strengthening the Imagination Through Theater: The Contributions of Michael Chekhov'. *Encounter: Education for Meaning and Social Justice* 21, no. 3 (2008): 8–15.

Chekhov, Michael. *Lessons for Teachers*, expanded edn. Light Rail, 2018.

Chekhov, Michael. *Lessons for the Professional Actor*. New York: Performing Arts Journal Publications, 1985.

Chekhov, Michael. *To the Actor on the Technique of Acting*. London: Routledge, 2002.

Chekhov, Michael. *The Path of the Actor*. London: Routledge, 2005.

Hagen, Uta. *A Challenge for the Actor*. New York: Simon & Schuster, 1991.

Hagen, Uta. *Respect for Acting*. New York: Macmillan Publishing, 1973.

Leonard, Charles. *Michael Chekhov's to the Director and Playwright*. New York: Limelight Editions, 1984.

MICHA. *Master Classes in the Michael Chekhov Technique*, DVD. London: Routledge, 2007.

Mitchell, Roanna. 'Something in the Atmosphere? Michael Chekhov, Deirdre Hurst Du Prey, and a Web of Practices between Acting and Dance'. *Theatre, Dance and Performance Training* 11, no. 3 (2020): 255–73.

Petit, Lenard. *The Michael Chekhov Handbook: For the Actor*. Oxford: Routledge, 2010.

Powers, Mala. *Michael Chekhov: On Theatre and the Art of Acting*, Audio CD. New York: Working Arts, 2004.

Ross, N. W. 'Foreword'. In *Miss Nellie: The Autobiography of Nellie C. Cornish*, edited by E. V. Browne and E. N. Beck, v–xiv. Seattle: University of Washington Press, 1965.

Shakespeare, William. *A Midsummer Night's Dream, The Arden Shakespeare Fifth Series*, edited by H. F. Brooks. New York: Routledge, 1988.

Shakespeare, William. *Hamlet: The Arden Shakespeare Third Series*, edited by A. Thompson and N. Taylor. London: Bloomsbury, 2016.

Stanislavski, Konstantin. *An Actor Prepares*, translated by Elizabeth Reynolds Hapgood. London: Methuen, 1994.

Steiner, Rudolf. *Colour*, translated by Pauline Wehrle. East Sussex: John Salter, 2001.

Strasberg, Lee. *A Dream of Passion: The Development of the Method*. New York: Penguin Putnam Inc., 1990.

WEB ADDRESSES

Michael Chekhov School of Acting: https://michaelchekhovschool.org/updates/

For on-demand classes with Ted Pugh and Fern Sloan go to: https://studio.michaelchekhovschool.org

MICHA, 'Masterclass videos': https://www.michaelchekhov.org/resources/masterclass-videos/. Micha's website allows you to digitally rent videos of classes in the Chekhov work.

Michael Chekhov: The Actor is the Theatre: https://collections.uwindsor.ca/chekhov/about. This website publishes a digital exhibition featuring an archive of approximately 3,600 typewritten pages documenting Michael Chekhov's work with the Chekhov Theatre Studio between 1936 and 1942.

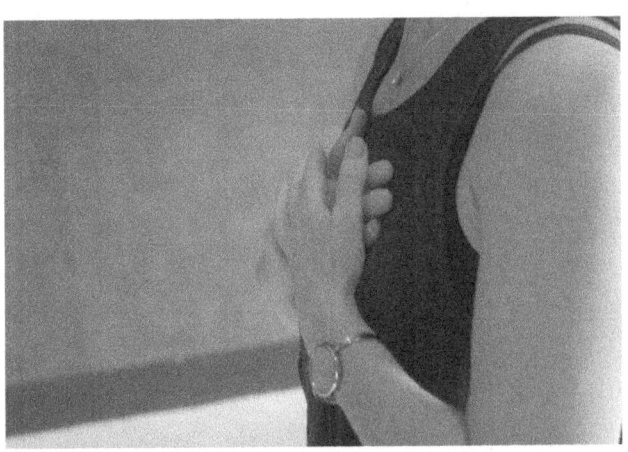

FIGURE 14 *Danielle Carter, 2015. Photography by Edward Marritz*

INDEX

Actors Ensemble 7–8, 76, 79, 180
Antigone 82, 83
archetypal gestures 167–8
archetypes 158–9
  deciding on 65–7
  exploration 64
  listening 65
  lists of 67–8
Arnold, Dawn 67
atmosphere
  collective imagination 57
  creation 60–1
  example 57–8
  objective 58–60
  personal 59–60
  qualities of movement 24
  relation to image 16
  sense of trust 58

Bonham-Carter, Victor 2
Bradbury, Ray 79
Bridgmont, Peter 6
The Brothers Karamazov 80

Caputo, Bethany 36–43
Chekhov, Anton 1
Chekhov, Michael xvi, xviii, 1–4, 6–8, 12–18, 20, 24, 26–8, 31, 33–9, 43, 45, 47, 50, 52, 54–8, 62–3, 65, 66, 69–73, 76, 77, 82, 85–7
Chekhov movement 8

Chekhov Studio 3, 6–7, 63
Chekhov technique
  Actors Ensemble 7–8
  balls as teaching tools 179–80
  collaboration 5–6
  Dartington ladies 1–3
  essentials (*see* essentials)
  misconceptions 174
  philosophy of 8–9
  receptive 174–5
  on to stage 86–7
  students to teachers 6–7
  teaching focus and concentration 175–6
  teaching images 177
  teaching imaginary body, centre and gesture 178–9
  teaching non-actors 177
  transformative tools (*see* transformative tools)
  work and studies 8
  working with young actors 176
  wrapping up 180–1
Chekhov Theatre School 2
class exercises
  archetypes 158–9
  awakening to gesture 160–4
  choices, contact and point of focus 168–70
  ensemble and objective atmosphere 149–51

INDEX

imaginary body 151–5
  for last week class 170
  mask to explore archetypal
    gestures 167–8
  personal atmosphere 145–9
  psychological gesture 165–6
  qualities of movement with
    tempo 135–7
  quality and sensation 139–43
  sensation with tempo 137–8
  staccato and legato 132–4
  stick, ball, veil 155–8
  straight lines and curves with
    imaginary centres
    128–31
  transformative tools 126–7
  'warm-up' classes 89
collaboration xvi–xvii 5–6
Conway, Merry 36, 39
creative potential, accessing
  through technique 8
Cutting, Blair 6

Dartington Hall 1–3, 20
*Dartington Hall: The formative
  years* 2
Dartington ladies 1–3, 7, 34,
  63
directions
  back-space 37, 119–20
  character development
    40–1
  character suggestion 37
  down 123–4
  first pass at a script 41
  front-space 37, 117–18
  gesture 40, 42
  movement 36, 43
  in and out 38–40, 121–2
  principle of 36
  sensing 42
  trajectories 41–2
  up 124–5
du Prey, Deirdre Hurst 1–3, 7

Elmhirst, Leonard 1
emotional life 4, 5, 13, 178
emotional response 98
ensemble atmosphere 60
essentials xviii, 11
  actor ideal centre 22–3
  crossing the threshold 18
  directions 36–43
  expanding and contracting
    19–22
  four brothers 26–9
  images 15–16
  inspired state 17–18
  listening 12–13
  psycho-physical 13–15
  qualities of movement 23–6
  radiating and receiving 29–33
  sensing and thinking 17
  tangible and intangible 16–17
  three centres 34–6
expanding and contracting 19–22
  opening and closing
    gestures 94–6
  space and periphery 90–1
exploration 26, 37, 64, 96, 151

Faison, Eleanor 3, 7
First Studio 2
floating (water) (Qualities of
  Movement) 23, 98–9,
  101
flying (air) (Qualities of
  Movement) 23, 99–100
*For the Pleasure of Seeing Her
  Again* 82
four brothers (ease, form, beauty,
  wholeness) 26–9, 103–6
free movement 116
Freidank, Ragnar xvi, xviii

gesture. *See also* psychological
  gesture
  directions and 40
  inner 18

The Grand Inquisitor 80
Grove, Eddie 6

Hagen, Uta 4, 5, 176, 179
Harper, Charles 7

ideal centre 22–3, 34–6
images 15–16, 61, 79–80, 85–6
imaginary body 82, 152–5
   moments of change 63–4
   physical, emotional, spiritual self 61
   playing with 62–3
   quality and substance for character 61
   trust subtle sensations 62
imaginary centres 81, 82
   choosing 47
   definition 46–7
   moving and changing 48–9
   working with 47–8
inner movement, of expanding 70, 92
inspired state 17–18

listening 12–13, 17, 30, 47, 65, 175

Mason, Felicity 3, 7
Meisner, Sanford 4
Merlin, Joanna xiii, 67
metronome 53, 54, 136, 138
Michael Chekhov Association (MICHA) xii, 8
Michael Chekhov School xvi, 8, 12
Michael Chekhov Studio 3–4, 6, 8, 20, 35
moulding (earth) (Quality of Movement) 23, 96–8, 101
Mrs Ripley's Trip 79, 82–4

objective atmosphere 58–60
On the Technique of Acting 3
outward movement 26, 38, 70, 137

performance 9, 28, 65, 66, 75, 80, 83, 85, 87, 136
personal atmosphere 59–60, 145–9
physical body 12–13, 27, 35, 62, 63, 100, 178–9
physical centres 34–6
physical, emotional and spiritual self 61, 179
The Possessed 3
psychological gesture 165–6
   development 69–72
   vs. movement 69
   use of 72–3
psycho-physical 13–15, 19, 24, 29, 36, 38, 117, 128
Pugh, Ted xvi–xviii, 3–9, 11–12, 14, 18, 20, 23, 25, 27, 29, 33–5, 42, 48, 50, 53–5, 57, 61, 62, 69–70, 73, 75–6, 80–7

qualities of movement 81
   floating (water), flying (air), moulding (earth), radiating (fire) 23–6, 96–101
   parts of body 25–6
   transitions between qualities 24–5, 102–3
quality and sensation 84, 139–43
   example of 54–5
   large packages of feelings/sensations 55–6
   personal feelings 55–6
   through will 56

radiating and receiving 107–12
throwing a ball 29–32

radiating (fire) (Quality of movement)   23–4, 100–1
rehearsals   29, 42, 64, 66, 75–8

script   15, 41
sensation   62
  quality and   54–6, 139–43
  with tempo   137–9
Sloan, Fern   xvi–xviii, 5, 7–9, 11–12, 14, 16–17, 23, 25, 27, 29, 34–5, 42, 48, 50, 53–5, 57, 61, 62, 69–70, 73, 75, 77, 79–86
Spellbound   3
Spoon River Anthology   7
staccato movement   50–2, 91
Stanislavski, Konstantin   2
Steiner, Rudolf   5–6
stick, ball and veil exercise   63, 155–8
Straight, Beatrice   1–3, 7
Straight, Willard   1

teaching   35
  balls as teaching tools   179–80
  focus and concentration   175–6
  images   177–8
  imaginary body, centre and gesture   178–9
  non-actors   177
tempo   42
  inner and outer   52–4
  qualities of movement with   135–7
  sensation with   137–9
Thompson, Ron   3

three centres (head, chest, will)   34–6, 114–16
tools to use
  camera work   85–6
  first read of play   78
  layering   80–4
  moments of change   86
  physical warm-up   76
  in rehearsal room   75–8
  roles   76
  technique   86–7
  working with images   79–80
  working with limited time   84–5
To the Actor   3, 4, 6, 16, 69–72, 128–31
touch and contact   112–13
trajectories, of forward and backward directions   125
transformative tools   xviii, 126–7
  archetype   64–8
  atmosphere   57–61
  definition   45
  imaginary body   61–4
  imaginary centres   46–9
  inner and outer tempo   52–4
  psychological gesture   69–73
  quality and sensation   54–6
  staccato and legato   50–2
The Trip to Bountiful   79

Whitney, Dorothy Payne   1
wholeness   28, 30, 181
Williamson, Glen   7
Witcover, Walt   5
wrapping up   180–1